BUSINESS ETHICS – FAITH THAT WORKS,

2ND EDITION

LEADING YOUR COMPANY TO LONG-TERM SUCCESS

LARRY RUDDELL

WESTBOW°
PRESS
A DIVISION OF THOMAS NELSON
& ZONDERVAN

Scripture taken from the New King James Version. Copyright © 1979, 1980, 1982 by Thomas Nelson, Inc. Used by permission. All rights reserved.

WestBow Press books may be ordered through booksellers or by contacting:

WestBow Press
A Division of Thomas Nelson & Zondervan
1663 Liberty Drive
Bloomington, IN 47403
www.westbowpress.com
1 (866) 928-1240

ISBN: 978-1-4908-5302-4 (sc)
ISBN: 978-1-4908-5303-1 (hc)
ISBN: 978-1-4908-5301-7 (e)

Library of Congress Control Number: 2014917311

Printed in the United States of America.

WestBow Press rev. date: 11/6/2014

To my students … thanks for your hard work and may you all live out your business ethics in an excellent manner to have an impact on many …

And to business leaders throughout the world, may these words start an ethical revolution that will result in unsurpassed blessings for the nations.

CONTENTS

TABLE OF FIGURES

ACKNOWLEDGMENTS

I WANT TO THANK MANY people for their help and support in putting together this book. I want to begin by thanking my good friend Ilhan from the Turkic World Presbyterian Church for encouraging me to write this book, and all his friends. Thanks to my faithful former colleague Al Williams who was the first to encourage me to publish (although a different book which God willing will come out in the future). I acknowledge Dr. Jay E. Adams whose accurate and practical use of Scripture greatly influenced me spiritually and influenced my writing style. I want to thank my students with whom I have hammered out many of these ideas. I also want to thank my good friend Professor Pat Thornton for providing a solid and encouraging atmosphere for developing ideas. My gratitude to South Shore Harbor Resort in League City, Texas for providing such a beautiful and peaceful atmosphere in which to write as well as Kusadasi Golf & Spa Hotel in western Turkey.

I received much help during the original editing process. Thanks to a number of students who examined my material: Maria Perez, Andie Scott, Analisse Orr, Tempie Smith, Perry King, Corey Barrett, Mandy Spakes, Patrick Uhlk, and Subhrata Barot. I want to particularly thank several students who provided detailed analysis and excellent suggestions: Tracy Taylor, Michael Rubash, Ashley Tate and **especially** Karen Ng. Professor Jason Smith was kind enough to review two new chapters of the 2nd edition. I also want to thank my brother Bill for his copious comments and particularly for correcting my free market faux pas.

My family was very supportive during this and other endeavors. I am thankful for my father Joe and mother Pat. My brothers serve as excellent ethical examples in their respective professions; Pres - lawyer, Jim - engineer and Bill - pilot. I am indebted to my lovely and gracious wife Aylin for her wonderful support during this ordeal and the hugs provided by my children Anna and Pres. They are both gifts to me.

I also want to thank God who does all things well. May He bless those who read this material to be a blessing as He wills.

Larry Ruddell
Houston, Texas
June, 2014

ABOUT THE AUTHOR

LARRY RUDDELL IS AN ASSOCIATE Professor in Business at Belhaven University and Dean of Faculty at Belhaven University, Houston campus. Dr. Ruddell graduated from Davidson College with a B.A. degree in Psychology. He then attended The Ohio State University where he received his M.A. in Counseling. After working for two years with the Dean of Students Office and as an Instructor at Sterling College in Kansas he completed his M.Div. Seminary Degree at Westminster Seminary in Philadelphia with an emphasis in counseling.

After moving to Houston, Dr. Ruddell was commissioned as a Chaplain in the United States Navy. He served three years of active duty with the Second Marine Division in Camp Lejeune, North Carolina, traveling to Norway, Okinawa, the Philippines, and Hong Kong. He then returned to Houston and completed his Ed.D. in Educational Leadership at the University of Houston with an emphasis on computer systems. His dissertation was on the topic: "Values in Leadership and Its Affect on Organizational Culture." Ruddell also earned his M.B.A. degree from the University of Houston – Clear Lake with an emphasis in Management.

Before moving into education, Dr. Ruddell worked for 12 years in the Houston area as a computer consultant in a number of different capacities including training, process analysis, database design and development, systems management, project management, and business development. He has worked for Nomos Systems, Inc. (as a founding partner), Quad S Consultants, Enron (with TCHD and OSI) and on a NASA contract with Booz, Allen & Hamilton. He has provided training and consulting for a number of companies (primarily through his own consulting company Integrated Systems and Services) including: Shell, Texaco, Senterra Development, Union Carbide, Baylor College of Medicine, Exxon, Pacific Gas and Electric (Houston), Lockheed-Martin, as well as at a Houston university (Strategic Planning). He is a Microsoft Certified Microsoft Access Trainer and has received his advanced certificate in Accelerated Learning. He has created a number of course curriculums for academic and training purposes as well as developed database applications.

Ruddell is the founder and president of the Global Institute for Ethical Leadership (GIEL), an organization established to "build good leaders for great organizations." Through GIEL, Dr. Ruddell has traveled to Turkey, Nepal, Indonesia and India delivering ethics programs and consultation to over 2,000 business, governmental and church leaders.

"…Beliefs drive strategy."
Tom Chappell, *Soul of a Business*

PREFACE

WHAT KIND OF COMPANY TO you want to build? Do you want to create a company that burns brightly like a spectacular firework, only to quickly fade in the night sky? Or do you want to create a company that explodes like a space rocket with enough force to travel to the far reaches of that night sky? You face more risk with the later approach. But the accomplishments of the rocket make the firework pale in comparison. I am convinced that this material on business ethics will help you soar as a leader and take your organization with you.

You are interested in ethics. You want to do the right thing. Yet, you also want to navigate your organization to success. This book is written to give you ideas that will help you understand your own business ethics and the ethics of others; and help you formulate a successful business ethics program to sustain long term positive financial performance. As Chappell (1993) highlights,

> ... Beliefs drive strategy. Your ethics can form the foundation of smart analysis and clear thinking. Your personal values can be integrated with managing for all the traditional goals of business - making money, expanded market share, increased profits, retained earnings, and sales growth. (p. xiv)

Many authors on business ethics have done a good job trying to address the practical ramifications of faith and business. However, it is difficult to give full attention to both. Some authors know business but they lack adequate theological training to address the faith issues.

Others understand theology, but they have a weak understanding of business. My desire in this book is to bring together in a real way **both** faith and business so you can see clearly how the two naturally fit together … seamlessly. Then you need to use this information to develop ethics in your organization for sustained success.

This book is for anyone, **especially leaders**, seeking to have a positive influence on his/her organization. It will help you make sense of the ethical issues in your organization (profit or non-profit). This book is also a great tool for training students in how to construct an effective business ethics program for their current or future organizations. I want to give you a competitive advantage. I want you to gain such a deep understanding of business ethics that you will know more than others. I want you to understand other people's positions so that you can make smart business decisions and steer clear of pitfalls. In this book, I show the ethical thought process for solving ethical problems and give specific examples. This will provide you with an ethical guideline for how to handle other kinds of issues. Then we go on to explore how to set up an effective ethics program so you can **prevent** those problems and do good to those around you.

This book demonstrates that faith is the foundation for the theory and practice of business ethics. As Dylan (1998) sang "you gotta serve somebody," so everyone has a belief that influences every decision they make. So you need to discover your faith (what you trust in to make life work) and the faith of others!

Chapter 1 covers some basic issues about business ethics including defining terms and describing how business ethics fits in with business strategy. This will give us a common understanding for our discussions in the rest of the book. It also addresses the motive driving ethics in most organizations and how to counter that motive. **Chapter 2** challenges readers to understand their own beliefs and actively base the ethics they develop and practice in business on those beliefs. It takes a leadership point of view and makes the point that ethics forms the foundation for effective leadership which forms the foundation for effective organizations. Chapter 2 also explores the two fundamental questions of ethics: what is your standard? and where does it come from?

Chapter 3 deals with the Christian view of business ethics. This will give you an example of how you might integrate your faith and life. I present an analysis of what the Scriptures teach about business ethics as a practical model of faith. This faith can (and indeed must) influence our business ethics. **Chapter 4** discusses the ethics of others and how to faithfully uphold standards in a diverse work situation. Secular standards for business ethics will then be presented and analyzed. Once we realize that belief plays a critical role in forming our business ethics, then what belief system works most effectively? Using the logic of C.S. Lewis (from *Mere Christianity*) that all people agree on common standards, we can then find that common standard for business ethics. Examples are used to illustrate how we can have one standard for an organization while allowing a diversity of ideas among the individuals in that organization. **Chapter 5** will cover issues of integration and practice within an organization, focusing on solving ethical problems. In this section, I will concentrate on how your ethical view frames all issues related to business ethics, even the issues you choose to call *ethical*. I give a couple of examples of how this approach works in dealing with ethical issues faced in business. We also present "steps for solving ethical problems" which can serve as a helpful guideline to organizations to make sure they respond effectively to organizational ethics issues. **Chapter 6** shows how to set up and carry out an effective ethics program for your business, in order to prevent ethical problems from occurring in the first place. Finally, **chapter 7** covers issues of integration and practice of business ethics outside the organization. This review of the modern concept of corporate social responsibility (CSR) will examine what it really means to help people and the environment and the particular role of business in that effort.

In summary, there are four major learning goals for the book; (1) that you understand your own ethics, (2) that you understand the ethics of others, (3) that you understand how to solve ethical problem and (4) that you understand how to set up an effective ethics program (both internally and externally). Treat these learning goals as a baseball game!

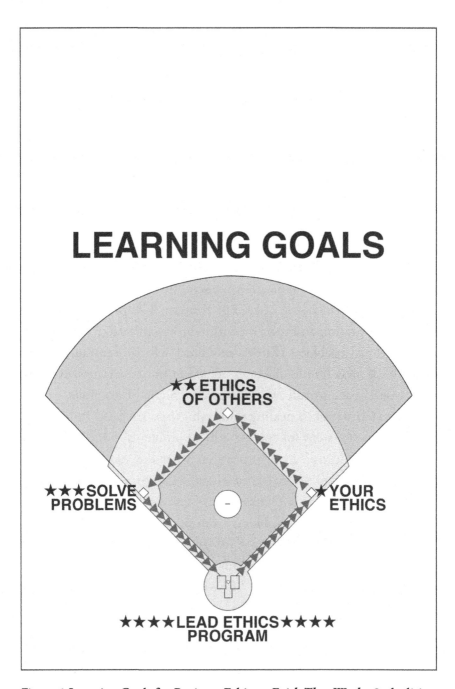

Figure 1 Learning Goals for Business Ethics – *Faith That Works*, 2nd edition

If you read this book and begin to understand your own ethics and can answer the two fundamental questions; what are your standards and where do they come from?; then that is a solid single and you have made progress! If you add to that knowledge an understanding of the ethics of others and the beliefs behind those ethics so you can function wisely in a diverse business environment, then that is a hard-hit double! Add to the first two an understanding of how to use your standard to solve specific ethical problems for yourself and your organization, then you have smacked a long triple! Finally, if you learn to prevent ethical problems by setting up an effective ethics program (along with the other three), then you have clouted a home run and have hit for the cycle! All the best as you step up to bat ... and keep your eye on the ball!

Chapter 1

BUSINESS ETHICS BASICS

BEFORE WE DISCUSS OUR BELIEF and work, let's lay out some basic concepts about business ethics. Again the purpose here is not to be exhaustive, but to communicate enough information for you to accurately understand ethics and their significance and effectively apply them.

First of all, business ethics is an application of ethics in general. That is what makes the study of business ethics so multi-faceted. You are really utilizing (among other things) the disciplines of philosophy, theology, and cultural study, not to mention business. This can prove challenging since few business people have studied ethics and probably fewer philosophers and theologians have studied business. So neither discipline has a deep enough view of the other to address issues in a holistic manner. Part of this problem can be attributed to our educational system (including of course colleges and universities). Students learn particular facts about the topics that they study. They learn facts about biology. They learn facts about psychology. They learn facts about history. However, they fail to learn how the facts relate with each other. They don't understand, for example, how Darwin's theory of evolution (assuming a naturalistic view of the world) framed some of the issues of interest to biology and even public policy in the 1900s.

This lack of integration carries over into MBA programs. The case study approach is used extensively. This method can be very useful as a means of applying thinking to real situations. This approach is needed. But, again if students have no universal principles to bring to bear on the cases, then answers become relative and can easily change in the

1

future, particularly regarding business ethics. Thus, the case study solutions become meaningless. Students could unwittingly be learning, for example, an evolutionary model for their ethical view that uses ethical words but has no real ethical meaning (regarding behavior) in real business situations. For example, as Etzioni (2002) reports, Harvard Business School was given $20 million in 1987 to support the teaching of ethics. After months of debate, a proposal was put forth to the faculty. They could not agree on how to approach the teaching of business ethics. One professor in particular suggested that there was no clarity as to whose values they would use, so there was no point in teaching business ethics. In the classroom, Etzioni (2002) was told,

> Ethics … were something a corporation simply cannot afford. Only if being moral bought the corporation "good will" - with a value that could be calculated and demonstrated - should the corporation take ethical considerations into account.

Ironically, Jeff Skillings, the architect of the Enron house of cards that fell in 2001 because of questionable ethical practices, was a graduate of Harvard Business School!

Let's now gain some perspective that will help us with integration by looking at the historical study of ethics. Ethics is considered a branch of philosophy. Under ethics, we find the topic of applied ethics, and business ethics is considered a part of applied ethics. We can diagram it this way:

```
PHILOSOPHY
     Metaphysics (the study of ultimate causes)
     Epistemology (study of how we know things)
     Ethics (study of what is right and wrong)
          - Normative Ethics (standards for right and wrong)
          - Applied Ethics (how we apply standards to specific situations)
               * Business Ethics
               * Sports Ethics
               * Medical Ethics
```

Figure 2 Business Ethics and Philosophy

The field of ethics is concerned with what is right and wrong, what is good and how we know what is right and good. The challenge is finding the standard by which we determine what is right and wrong. Thus, the field of ethics is intimately connected with metaphysics (or worldview), specifically ontology (a category of metaphysics) or the study of being. Where do we come from? Why are we here? What is our purpose? Where are we going after death? How do we arrive at our standard of right and wrong? You might say that metaphysics determines the foundation or reason for judging right and wrong.

How does this philosophical musing apply to real decisions in business ethics? What is the universal idea that we embrace that helps us make sense out of the particular situations that we face in life?[1] This can be illustrated in the following diagram:

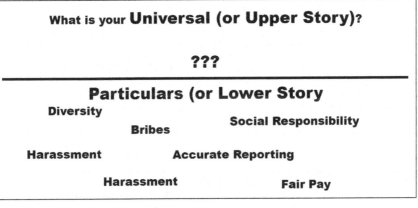

Figure 3 Universals and Particulars (Schaeffer, 2006)

As we make choices in the day to day situations that we face (or Particulars), why do we make these choices and not others? For example, some of the particular choices we are faced with in business might

---

[1]   Also, see Aristotle's (circa 340 B.C.) comments, "Now of Justs and Lawfuls each bears to the acts which embody and exemplify it the relation of a universal to a particular; the acts being many but each of the principles only singular because each is universal."

include: How hard do I work? What do I do about handling money? How am I going to compete? As you answer these questions, you should then ask the question; Why did I make these choices? This helps us determine our Universal, the standard that guides our day-to-day decision-making. This discussion should prepare you to answer at least the second of the two questions (discussed in the next chapter): Where do my standards come from?

Now that we have a brief peek at the philosophical context of our discussion, let's move ahead with more specific definitions.

DEFINITIONS

There are two basic points of view when considering definitions related to business ethics[2]:

1. **Theistic** - Truth and ultimate standards are unchanging and come from a Supreme Being outside ourselves.
2. **Secularistic** - Truth comes from within and there are no ultimate standards beyond ourselves: "Ethics is autonomous and situational, needing no theological or ideological sanction. Ethics stems from human need and interest. ... critical intelligence, infused by a sense of human caring, is the best method that humanity has for resolving problems" (Kurtz, 1973, pp. 17-18).

---

[2] See Romans 1:18-19 where we have the Theistic view presented, "For the wrath of God is revealed from heaven against all ungodliness and unrighteousness of men, who by their unrighteousness suppress the truth. For what can be know about God is *plain to them*, because God *has shown it to them*" (ESV) (emphasis added). Romans 1:22-23 continues with the Secularistic view, "Claiming to be wise, they became fools, and *exchanged the glory of the immortal God for images resembling mortal man ...*" (ESV) (emphasis added).

Personal preference is the standard here (autonomous and situational), and there is no unchanging standard apart from us.[3] Obviously, there are many variations of these basic types. The different views that we will discuss later draw from one of these basic perspectives.

As we can see, one of the challenges in discussing business ethics is that there is disagreement about the meaning of the terms involved. In fact, it is humorous at times to hear people discuss the topic of business ethics when they really are not sure what the terms mean. To compensate for a lack of clarity, speakers heap up words in hopes that one will stick. So you hear people talk about the ethics, morals, values, and standards of their company; without really understanding the meanings of any of these terms.

One of the challenges many societies face today is that the meaning of words changes.[4] This is not a problem in itself. For example, the word *mouse* obtained an entirely new meaning in the 1980s with the advent of the graphical user interface (GUI) on our computer screens and the input device used to select things on those screens. However, even that meaning is growing obsolete as we shift to *touch screens* for our input devices and *text* is no longer something you write as a paper but a message you send from your phone. This is to be expected as new items are introduced into society and we use old, meaningful terms to

---

[3] George (2001) is more direct about the nature of this two-fold conflict: "The clash of worldviews characteristically pits morally conservative Jews, Christians, and other believers against secular liberals and those who, though remaining within religious denominations, have adopted liberal ideas about personal and political morality. Orthodox Jews, conservative and evangelical Protestants, faithful Catholics, and eastern Orthodox Christians [and I would add some Muslim groups] today find themselves allied with one another in defending, say, the sanctity of human life or the traditional concept of marriage against their liberal co-religionists who have joined forces with secularists of various stripes to support such things …" (p. xiii) (brackets added).

[4] Of course, the basic goal of *propaganda* is to mislead people, often by using familiar words but injecting new meanings into them. The idea is to make everything appear "normal" while ripping out the previous worldview and replacing it with another one without openly and honestly presenting the different worldview on its own terms.

identify them. The problem comes when we inject new meanings into words that have to do with the standards by which we behave. Words are meant to clarify understanding, not to confuse. For example, in Genesis 1:3 we read "And God said, 'Let there be light,' and there was light." There is no distinction between the word and reality; speaking and action. This is the way communication was intended. Jesus is called the Word in John 1, which means He accurately reflects God (and is God!) in His words and actions ... they are seamless.[5] This is the model for communication in the world.

When people use words improperly (again regarding the standards by which we live), then listeners are confused. See 2 Corinthians 4:1-2 where Paul contrasts his purpose in communication with the misleading communication of his opponents:

> Therefore, having this ministry by the mercy of God, we do not lose heart. But we have renounced disgraceful, underhanded ways. We refuse to practice cunning or to tamper with God's word, but by the open statement of the truth we would commend ourselves to everyone's conscience in the sight of God. (ESV)

When assaulted with misleading communication, people think they hear one thing, but the communicator means something different. This is a pernicious deception, as George Orwell described in his book 1984. Think about it. How can you build a solid ethical foundation when you can't even use ethical terms in an ethical manner! Sproul (1986) summarizes the problem, "This proliferation of options [regarding the meaning of ethics] generates confusion, and, for many, a sense of despair about reaching a cultural consensus that would stabilize the shifting

---

[5] See also Hebrews 1:3: "He is the radiance of the glory of God and the exact imprint [or consistent and accurate representation] of his nature [being; exactly who He is] ..." (ESV) (brackets added).

sands of pluralism"[6] (p. 8) (brackets added). Thus, it is critical to define terms clearly and then use them consistently. Let's crisply define several terms now that are germane to our clear understanding of business ethics. Keep in mind that I am attempting to capture the original and purest form of each word. It is important that you properly understand the words even if others do not.

Let's begin by talking about *worldview* (also called big belief, schema, underlying assumption or meta belief). Your worldview is basically your metaphysics (as discussed in the previous chapter). "A worldview is a set of assumptions we hold (consciously or subconsciously) about the basic makeup of our world" (Sire, 1976, p. 17). This involves answers to the questions: What is our ultimate purpose? Where did we come from? How can we know things? What happens when we die? Does truth come from outside us or does truth come from within? Understanding your perspective towards these big issues is critical to understanding your foundation for business ethics. To highlight the importance of worldview; your worldview actually influences your definition of the ethical terms we are discussing right now! Your worldview answers the second fundamental business ethics question, "where does your standard come from"?

As Adams (1983) describes (based on Scriptural analysis), the *heart* is the seat of your personality. We often think of heart as a contrast to head. So, for example you can think something (your mind) but it is perhaps more important to feel something (your heart). But the heart is not just emotions. This is a Roman, western romantic notion of who we are. In reality, the heart is the sum of all that is going on inside us including thoughts, feelings, conscience, and motives. It is contrasted with words and actions (what we actually say and do), NOT what we

---

[6] This is a concept that is particularly true in academia. University Professors often posit their work as *scholarship* when they are simply injecting *new meaning* into old concepts. Instead of simply using and discussing the changing **applications** of a word, new meanings are created or a new word is invented to describe an old concept.

think.[7] Thinking is an internal activity, part of the activity of the heart. The heart is also the seat of faith, determining what we ultimately trust in. In business ethics, it is important to obtain consistent agreement between our heart (who we really are on the inside) and our actions. For example, applying to business, there needs to be alignment between the mission, how it is communicated and how it is executed operationally. It is important to understand the meaning of the word heart because if a company wants to effectively engender business ethics in its people, it must take the heart into consideration.[8]

Now let's define the term ***ethics***. Ethics are the **universal** and **unchanging** standards of what we **should** do; what is **good**. Another, more specific, way to say it (from a Christian worldview) is that ethics are simply God's Word applied to specific situations.[9] Notice that this definition appeals to standards beyond us. Appealing to individual preferences as a standard for ethics renders ethical discussions

---

[7] See Matthew 15:8 where people honor God with their lips, but their heart is far from him. See 1 Samuel 16:7 where man looks at the outward appearance but God looks at the heart. See 1 Peter 3:4 where the inner life of individuals is called the "hidden person of the heart." The inner person is the one that the Lord alone knows - it is hidden from the rest of us; we look only at the outer man. That is one major reason why we must never judge a man's motives: we simply don't know what they are. Rather, we must judge only his actions and his words (i.e., those factors that **are** accessible to us). (This information is from Adams, 1983, p. 4).

[8] See chapters 5 and 6 about the importance of implementing a *values* based approach to business ethics in organizations (you might say a "heart" based approach) vs. simple compliance (just keeping the bare minimum of the law).

[9] Of course this is not always easy. Sin complicates life, including our own ability to see things accurately. This is an ongoing effort to see the situation accurately based on God's perspective and apply the proper Scripture in that situation. This is indeed a work of the Holy Spirit. See 2 Timothy2:14-15: "Remind them of these things, and charge them before God not to quarrel about words, which does no good, but only ruins the hearers. Do our best to present yourself to God as one approved, a worker who has no need to be ashamed, *rightly handling the word of truth*." (ESV) (emphasis added) It is not enough to know about the Bible but we need to apply it accurately. See also Matthew 5:17 ff. where Jesus correctly interprets and applies Old Testament passages.

meaningless because everything is relative. We will talk more about this issue later in the book. Ethics comes from the Greek word *ethos* and stands for the philosophical discipline of exploring the Good or what is right. As Sproul (1986) points out, it was,

> ... derived from the root word meaning "stall," a place for horses. It conveyed the sense of a dwelling place, a place of stability and permanence. ... Ethics is a normative science, searching for the principal foundations that prescribe obligations or "oughtness." It is concerned primarily with the imperative and with the philosophical premises upon which imperatives are based. (p. 9)

Morals are the standards that we adopt from a particular **group** at a particular time based on what people **actually do** (Sproul, 1986). It is more a sociological term from the Roman Latin term *mores* or customs. People look around them to see what people are doing and then formulate standards from the behavior.[10]

It is important to understand the distinction between these two terms: **ethics** and **morals**. In many cases, people use the term business ethics when they really mean morals. Morals are relative to situations and personal preferences. So, if a company has a moral code, you can bet that this code may change. Unfortunately, many people add to the confusion by using the term morals when they really are talking about ethics. It is important to clarify terms. Ideally, one's ethics and morals should be the same (in other words, the behavioral culture of an organization reflects universal standards). But, in most cases this is not true. This confusion can lead to people give up what they know is right in order to "fit in" with whatever the current group is doing due to peer pressure.

---

[10] See Aristotle's comment (circa 340 B.C.), "... the Moral comes from custom, so the Greek term denoting it is but a slight deflection from the term denoting *custom* in that language."

When people act in ways that violate their ethical standards while doing business, they have a choice. They can realize they are wrong and correct their behavior to come back in line with the ethical standard they know is true, or they can do just the opposite. They can justify their actions and conclude that their ethical standards must be wrong. So, they moralize by redefining their moral standards (based on what they have done) and then (this is where the problem arises) redefine the universal ethical standards to fit their current actions. This is profoundly illustrated at the end of the movie: Crimes and Misdemeanors. The lead character (Martin Landeau) is discussing his life, since he had his lover murdered, with the character played by Woody Allen. Allen suggests that Landeau should feel guilty about this event and turn himself in. Landeau states just the opposite; that his life is now perfectly normal and that to feel guilty about the past events is not real. Reality (to him) is acting like it did not happen. This is a shift by the lead character from his initial reaction to the crime when he felt very bad (because of his religious upbringing). You could say that he had a shift in worldview in response to what he did where the ultimate standard became his own peace and contentment instead of the ultimate standards of a living God where adultery and murder are unacceptable.

As we will see later, the problem is further complicated by the fact that people want to hold others accountable to the universal ethical standards (not their own, lower standards).[11] In other words, they want the standards changed for themselves, but not others. Sometimes an organization has consistent **unethical** standards. In other words, they have changed the meaning of the word ethics to fit their moral standards (what is actually going on). I think these organizations will run into problems in the long run even though they may experience harmony in the short run. As Sproul (1986) states, "Morals describe what people do;

---

[11] Actually this is a specific technique used in social activism (Alinsky, 1971); to radically hold others to their own standards and accuse them when they fall short (as everyone will) and in the process, erode those standards in culture; while holding themselves accountable to no ethical standards.

ethics define what people ought to do. The difference between them is the norm and the normative:

Ethics	Morals
1. Normative	1. Descriptive
2. Imperative	2. Indicative
3. Oughtness	3. Isness
4. Absolute	4. Relative

Figure 4 Meaning of *Ethics vs. Morals*

When morality is identified with ethics, the normal becomes the normative and the imperative is swallowed by the status quo" (p. 10).

A ***value*** is "An assessment of worth (gained from past influences) and expressed in our life choices" (Stayton, 1986). More simply put, values are "whatever you think is important." So, in some ways, it is ethically meaningless to have a values statement for your company. However, if the company values right and wrong (ethics), then the values statement (or statement of core values) can make sense. Your values can also reflect what is important to you as a company strategically.

RUDDELL'S MODEL

One of the challenges of business ethics is that you must understand ethics **and** business. You must understand what you believe and you must understand your business enough to know what **should** be done in various aspects of the business. If you are ignorant of the business, then you won't know that you are violating a standard. It is helpful to think about it this way: if you were starting up your own business, what would be your ethics statement? What are the particular ethical issues that you face in your particular organization/industry? How would you apply your views to particular ethical issues in your business? How would you let others know about your views in ways that impact them?

Another challenge of business ethics is that you must understand your own ethics **and** the ethics of others and also the ethics of the organization in which you are involved. Most people think of handling ethical interactions in business in terms of compromise. But when it comes to your ethical standards, you should never compromise.[12] A better way to look at ethical interactions is in terms of honesty and respect. You want others to be honest about their ethics and you respect their point of view and take them seriously. But that doesn't mean that you have to agree with them. Let's explore this dynamic further!

Having a successful global business means understanding your own view and also the views of others, including the views of the organization so that you can find a common ground for doing business. A common ground for doing business is the ethical area where you can agree with the ethics of **others**[13] and/or the ethics of the **organization** in a business transaction or task WITHOUT GIVING UP YOUR OWN STANDARDS! Perhaps the challenges of managing the three sets of ethics involved in a business decision are best summed up in the following diagram:

---

[12] Keep in mind that is important NOT to be legalistic here (see chapter 5). We are talking about genuine ethical issues such as stealing, dealing falsely with another, et al. ... core items of right and wrong.

[13] The "ethics of others" includes everyone that you might have to do business; people within your organization and those outside your organization including (for example) fellow-workers, customers, vendors, governmental personnel, and people in the surrounding community.

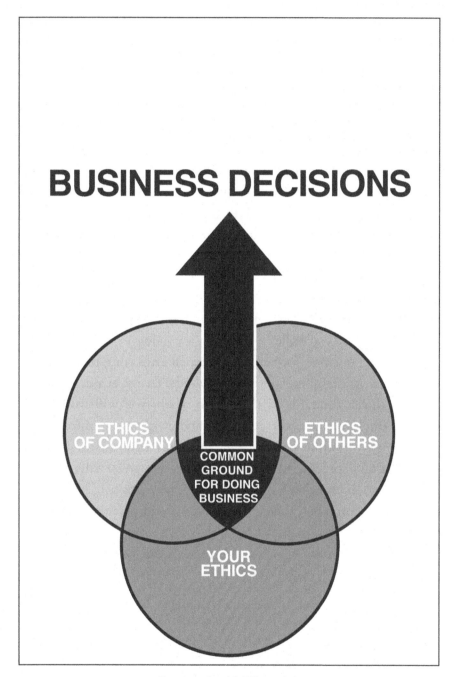

Figure 5 Ruddell's Model

Keep in mind that these interactions take place in **Reality**; the way the universe actually runs, we might say the "**real** reality." Our **worldview** is how we view reality (see definition of worldview earlier in chapter). This forms the foundation for our ethical views. **Reality** does not change even though our views may change

Let's examine the diagram. We have three different ethical perspectives: ethics of the **organization, personal** ethics, and ethics of **others**. **Ethics of the organization** are the standards found in the ethics statement of the organization. This may be called different things such as ethics statement, code of conduct,[14] values (or core values), or core beliefs.[15] This is important to know because hopefully there is a consistency between the stated ethics of the organization and the ethics of the key leaders in that organization. If the stated ethics of the organization do not reflect the ethics of the key leaders, then there is a problem. **Personal ethics** are YOUR ethics. This is perhaps the main point of this book; that you think through what YOU believe. If you don't know what you believe, then you are going to have a difficult time figuring out the views of others, much less trying to work with them while maintaining your own standards. Lastly, **ethics of others** are the ethical standards of those with whom you will work. This includes employees, vendors, customers and people in the surrounding community, including government. You must take their views into consideration in order to work effectively; otherwise you will not find a common ground for doing business. The main point here is that your ethics are important in the equation. As we said previously, business

---

[14] Although, technically a code of conduct is the application of ethical standards.

[15] Many companies simply have a *code of conduct*, which explains in detail (normally) what people are NOT to do, often for legal reasons. However, without appealing to any standards, the code of conduct can easily lead to legalism or *loopholism* (see chapter 5). See Paul's argument in Galatians 4:8-11 about the problem of simply "following rules" without any higher, ethical purpose. It is OK to have a code of conduct, but each part should refer to the company ethics statement and the code should detail what people SHOULD do (based on organizational standards) when faced with an ethical issue common to the industry and an individual's particular function within the organization.

ethics must be based not on compromise but honesty and respect. You should not have to "toss your ethics over the side" in order to please the company or a customer, for example.[16]

This is where we need to make an important distinction between **tolerance** and **pluralism** when it comes to working with the ethics of others and the organization. Tolerance means that you respect people and their ideas. You treat people with care. You show good will towards all people, even those with whom you disagree. This is healthy in any organization. This is important. This is good. Pluralism, on the other hand, means that all ideas are equally valid. This is not necessary and is rationally untenable. As Joel Betz (2001) states:

> That's why I've always tried to make a clear distinction between "tolerance" on the one hand, and "pluralism" on the other. "Tolerance" gives me room to say, "I think you're wrong, but I'll defend your right to be wrong." "Pluralism" suggests, much more strongly than most folks admit, that there isn't any such thing as right and wrong and no such thing as truth and error. As it is practiced more and more in America, pluralism tends to require that you not only leave room for your neighbor to believe what he believes, but that you also refrain from disagreeing with it. There's a world of difference between the two perspectives.
>
> Tolerance promotes civility combined with clear thinking. Pluralism promotes civility [and we could add acquiescence] combined with mushy-headedness. That's not just my conclusion. My desk dictionary includes a definition for "pluralism" that calls it a "theory that reality is composed of

---

[16] In fact, it should be just the opposite. See Hebrews 12:1-2 where we are instructed to "toss our sinful patterns over the side," "... let us lay aside every weight, and sin which clings so closely, and let us run with endurance the race that is set before us, looking to Jesus ..." (ESV).

a multiplicity of ultimate beings, principles, or substances. Dualism." (brackets added)

As the Law of Non Contradiction reminds us, something cannot be true and not true at the same time. Schaeffer (1968) applies this notion to ethics. He reminds us that a new way of looking at truth has affected us. "The tragedy of our situation today is that men and women are being fundamentally affected by the new way of looking at truth and yet they have never even analyzed the drift [which he call the fog] which has taken place" (p. 13) (brackets added). Schaeffer (1968) goes on to state,

> The basic one [presupposition] was that there really are such things as absolutes. They accepted the possibility of an absolute in the area of Being (or knowledge), and in the area of morals. ... So if anything was true, the opposite was false. ... We must not forget that historic Christianity stands on a basis of antithesis. Without it historic Christianity is meaningless. (pp. 14-15) (brackets added)

An action cannot be moral and immoral at the same time.

This is somewhat akin to what happens with diversity. You need to understand other points of views. You need to show tolerance for people with different views but not necessarily from a pluralistic perspective. In other words you don't have to adopt or agree with that other view. The whole point of ethics is to distinguish between good and bad. Otherwise, the word ethics does not have a real meaning (which, unfortunately is the case in some secular ideologies. We will explore this concept in more detail in the next chapter).

Now, let's shift our focus. Let's look at ethics from the business perspective. After all, it does little "good" for businesses to do the right thing if they cannot make any money. How can ethics impact the bottom line?

STRATEGIC VALUE OF BUSINESS ETHICS

"Business is Business" (Problem)

Let's consider the business reasons for focusing on business ethics. Many companies have a statement of ethics. Some key leaders of these organizations may talk enthusiastically about ethics. But, the fact remains that when decisions have to be made in the thick of the actual transactions of business, many leaders toss their ethical statements over the side and act by the credo: *business is business*. The slogan *business is business* means that business is so competitive that others will take advantage of you if you try to act ethically, so you **have** to go against your "normal ethics" and use different ethics in business. The rationalization is that you are *sympathetic to acting ethically*. You are basically a *good* person. You really believe that *you don't want to do the wrong thing,* but *circumstances dictate it. Everyone else is doing it*; so in order to compete you must follow suit. You don't fight it, because *business situations are different from the rest of life.* You have to act differently. After all, b*usiness is business.*

The point leaps out that at bottom line, many leaders don't really believe that conducting business ethically will increase the profit and success of the company. Most see ethics as a constraint on profits (Bowie, 1988). The fact is, however, that companies that set and hold to ethical standards will do better financially and be able to compete more effectively than unethical companies **in the long run**. I would argue that in many cases, one of the reasons that businesses are tempted to act unethically is because they have not done a proper job in planning strategically. The way to attack the *business is business* mindset is to convince people (and yourself!) that ETHICS ARE GOOD FOR BUSINESS.[17]

---

[17] Notice there are numerous reasons why ethics are good for business in the following section. The Scripture sometimes uses "overkill" to make a point abundantly clear

Why Ethics are Good for Business (Solution)

Let's look at some of the reasons why ethics are critical for business success. First of all, in order for an organization to run consistently, **some** standard needs to be followed. If there is no consistent standard, then chaos results. As Cavanagh (1998) asserts, "...without a value system or ideology, it is impossible to make consistent and reasonable decisions" (p. 2).

There are other reasons why business ethics are good for business. Norman Bowie (1988) highlights several reasons. Conducting an ethical business reduces the cost of business transactions (such as delivery of goods by supplier and payment for those goods) by encouraging prompt payments particularly by large companies to small vendors. Internal costs are reduced when employees are working hard, not taking drugs, and not stealing. Productivity is maximized and employees can be trusted to do what they say they will do. Conducting an ethical business establishes trust among stakeholders (all people affected by a business activity). Profit is more likely when a company exhibits ethical behavior. When the people in a company act ethically, they develop a positive reputation. This reputation will tend to draw customers, employees, and suppliers who are also ethical. "Thus trust is reinforcing in a kind of virtuous circle" (Bowie, 1988, p. 2). This kind of company will gain a competitive advantage in the long run by being seen as keeping its word and not taking advantage of others. Internally, the Personnel function will be streamlined so there is less policing and more mentoring. This reduces paperwork and allows energy to be more focused on building the organization rather than having to accommodate poor performance. Also numbers will be reported accurately. This allows investors to know exactly where the company stands instead of providing a false view based on cooked books. For example, employee and company leadership relationships could be much improved if the employees knew that the salaries of the key leaders were not overly exorbitant.

(i.e. many examples of faith in Hebrews 11). That is needed here because the *business is business* mindset can be so entrenched.

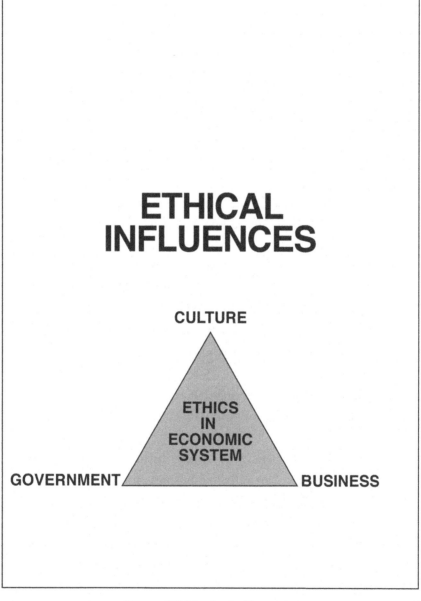

Figure 6 Ethics in the Economy

Conducting an ethical business preserves social capital so that the free market system can continue to operate. You can say that business ethics is the **foundation** of the free market system. Without business ethics, you lose the heart of the capitalistic system. Note the diagram and how business (along with government and culture) all have an ethical obligation to fill if the economy will prosper. In previous generations, business could simply react to the ethics of culture and government to "maintain the status quo." But, now businesses need to rise to the challenging of being a positive ethical influence on culture themselves.

Let's explore other reasons why ethics is good for business. Hoffman (1995) lists the following as reasons why business ethics are important:

1. At the very least, a solid ethical foundation is effective in establishing limits on conduct that is not proscribed by laws and regulations.
2. A program of ethics initiatives is definitely in the self-interest of every company and employee today. White-collar crime is conservatively estimated to cost businesses well in excess of $100 billion per year. ... also bankruptcies, lost jobs, restructuring, declining stock values of companies that have been involved in ethical lapses.
3. Institutions are discovering that an effective ethics program sets the tone for a superior corporate culture. ... high level of trust and candor.
4. Ethics initiatives have a positive influence in the realm of relationships. ... an effective business tool when so much of commerce involves preserving and strengthening relationships among customers, employees, suppliers, regulators and investors.
5. Ethics provides employees at all levels with the leadership skills they need, as organizations require autonomous decision making from them.
6. A solid moral foundation gives companies a competitive edge. (pp. 233-234)

Carter McNamara (2000) lists ten benefits of managing ethics in the workplace (eight of which are listed here):

1. Attention to business ethics has substantially improved society by addressing poor work conditions and fairness in competition.
2. Ethics programs help maintain a moral course in turbulent times so that there is consistency in leadership behavior no matter what the circumstances.
3. Ethics programs cultivate strong teamwork and productivity by encouraging alignment between the stated ethics of the organization and the actual actions of key leaders and other employees thus developing teamwork and unity of purpose.
4. Ethics programs support employee growth and meaning so that employees face reality (good and bad) and know where they stand within organizations.
5. Ethics programs are an insurance policy - they help insure that policies are legal.
6. Ethics programs help avoid criminal acts of omission by encouraging individuals in organizations to be proactive in identifying and facing ethical problems rather than avoiding and covering up.
7. Ethics programs help manage values associated with quality management, strategic planning and diversity management so that qualities needed to make the business successful are developed by all.
8. Ethics programs promote a strong public image, which is good for further business. (pp. 4-6)

Mary Campbell (n.d.) suggests six reasons why business ethics are good for business:

1. People prefer to do business with trustworthy companies.
2. Employees remain longer and work more productively if their employers are honest and fair.

3. Employees are quicker to steal from unethical employers than principles ones.
4. Fines and legal settlements can destroy small businesses and cripple large ones.
5. Regulators are less likely to investigate companies known for fairness.
6. Training tells employees the company means business.

Leadership theory tends to attribute success to leaders who improve financial performance and handle people effectively, thus leading to successful organizations. Financial performance can be improved in two basic ways: reducing costs and increasing revenue. People management includes not only employees but also others (vendors, customers, stockholders, and other people in society). Let's categorize the above benefits to underscore the positive **financial** results of ethical leadership, thus illustrating how ethics are "good for business."

Reduces Costs

1. Reduces the cost of business transactions by encouraging prompt payments particularly by large companies to small vendors.
2. Employee cost is reduced when employees work hard. Working hard means that each individual is producing close to their maximum capability. This makes production more efficient and lowers labor costs because more people are not needed to make up for the lack of productivity of current employees.
3. Employees are not stealing. This minimizes shrinkage, thus cutting costs.
4. Employees are not taking illegal drugs. This reduces costs from employees missing work (due to drug influence or rehabilitation programs), performing in an ineffective manner, causing accidents, or going to court or jail because of taking illegal substances.
5. Internally, the Personnel function will be streamlined so there is less policing and more mentoring. This reduces paperwork and

allows energy to be more focused on building the organization rather than having to accommodate poor performance. This reduces costs.

6. Productivity is maximized because employees can be trusted to do what they say they will do. This reduces costs and allows growth.

7. Employees remain longer and work more productively if their employers are honest and fair. This reduces cost of training new people and increases productivity because experienced people are the ones doing the work.

Increases Sales

1. People are more likely to buy from ethical companies and conduct repeat business and tell others about the company.

2. Ethical companies will tend to develop good will that results in a higher value for investors

3. Improvements in quality because employees will do things right the first time and follow through. This adds value to products or services that can allow higher prices.

4. When the people in a company act ethically, the company develops a positive reputation. This reputation will tend to draw customers, employees, and suppliers who are also ethical.

5. Conducting an ethical business establishes trust among stakeholders (all people affected by a business activity). This increases likelihood that others will do business in an excellent manner with your company.

6. Numbers will be reported accurately. This allows investors to know exactly where the company stands instead of providing a false few based on cooked books.

7. Attention to business ethics has substantially improved society by addressing poor working conditions and fairness in competition.

8. Positive influence for good on all peoples connected with the company, which will develop society for good.

9. Able to grow - banks willing to loan to honest companies

Ethics and Strategy

Because ethics leads to success, ethics should permeate all aspects of the organization, including strategic planning. Unfortunately this is often not the case. Ethics are added as an after thought in order to comply with legal mandates. I spoke with the compliance officer and one of his associates from a large corporation in the southwest United States about their organizational and functional roles. Often times, the ethics group is assigned to Personnel or reports directly to corporate leaders in a staff role. In this case these two individuals were attached to the Legal department. Apparently the corporation's main reason for having the compliance office was to minimize lawsuits. It was a means for risk management. This is OK in helping to avoid some problems. But it does not go far enough. There should also be a proactive (or values based) focus on personal responsibility and how to do the right thing in real situations.[18]

The relationship between business ethics and strategic planning can be summarized below:

1. It is a way to develop trust among employees, customers, suppliers, investors, and with the community.
2. It fosters cooperation and innovation within the organization.
3. It focuses on the **long term**, which is the perspective needed for ethics to pay off.
4. There is an incentive to stay ethical due to government penalties for repeat offenders and leadership knowledge.
5. Including ethics in strategic planning makes sure that doing good is proactive as well as reactive. Corporate ethical behavior and good financial performance go together.
6. It highlights the importance of the relationship between the Board and the CEO.

---

[18] See a further discussion of this dynamic in chapter 5.

7. Developing a code of ethical conduct influences the goals of the organization which will determine exact plans for reaching the goals.

8. Ethics as a standard for strategic planning; affects ALL aspects of the operation. (Cavanagh, 1998, pp. 245-259)

Trust comprises the absolute foundation of all business transactions. If there is no trust, there can be little productive business activity. There needs to be trust that companies will deliver the products they say they will deliver at the agreed upon price, quantity, and quality; and that the agreed upon payments will be made. If trust is not present (or is violated), then all that remains is raw power and deceit and greed. As Chewning, Eby, & Shirley (1990) put it,

> Just think what it would be like if everyone were honest, as God intended. ... Businesses would not need to spend money to protect themselves from shoplifters. Customers could know that advertisements give honest information and that product claims were true. (p. 42)

Business strategists talk about the important role of organizational culture in sustaining a competitive advantage. You can have a strong mission and a well-developed strategy for winning in your market, but if you don't build your organizational culture effectively to execute that strategy, then you will fail in the long run. This dynamic might be best illustrated by a train.

Figure 7 Business Ethics and Strategy

The train is pursuing a destination (its vision) by moving down the tracks (implementing its mission). The train needs fuel to move (capital) and this (along with resulting profits) tends to garner the attention of most businesses. There is nothing wrong with this financial focus, but note the diagram and how the financial focus (with the CFO in charge of this area of the business) tends to dominate the diagram, which is what can happen in real organizations. But if you look closely at the diagram, there is a problem. The track is in disrepair. This will, at best, make the train slow down, which means a disruption in moving forward with the mission due to organizational concerns and inefficiencies. At worst, the train could derail and still "go fast" as it bounces into the countryside until it invariably crashes and burns.

The track is the business ethics of the organization. You may not notice the ethics (as in our diagram), but there are always some ethics operating in the organization and if they are bad, they can seriously disrupt an organization. Since your organizational ethics form the core of your organizational culture, it behooves you as a leader to pay attention to developing those ethical standards (see chapters 5 and 6 of this book) and making sure they are upheld in every aspect of the organization. But, let's be more specific. Why is this so difficult?

Chewning, Eby, & Shirley (1990) cite an article regarding college freshmen and their views of what is most important in life:

> A recent study of 209,000 college freshmen [from Kreider, Carl. (1980). "A Christian Standard of Living," in The Christian Entrepreneur. Scottsdale, PA: Herald Press. Chapter 5] discovered that 75.6 percent listed "being very well off financially" as an essential or very important goal. (p. 12) (brackets added)

These results are not surprising. If college freshmen think this, then we could venture that most business people would think it even more. Money is where it's at. What you think about money and what you think it will do for you in the long run is critical to your perspective on business ethics. Think about it right now. Deep down, what do you want money to do for you? How much money would it take? What kind of peace and contentment would it bring? We will talk more about this dynamic later in the book,[19] but seriously consider a different focus. If you develop a meaningful philosophy of life (based on your worldview) and act on it, this will best equip you to do the right thing AND carry out a successful business (in the long run). Let's move on to the next chapter and explore further!

---

[19] See chapter 3 and why a large part of Scriptural analysis in that chapter confronts this mindset with the Biblical one.

CHAPTER 1 QUESTIONS FOR REVIEW

1. Why is the study of business ethics said to be "multi-faceted"? What does that mean and what difference does that make for you?

2. How does the study of ethics fit in with philosophy? How does this help you understand the study of ethics and help you figure out your standard for right and wrong?

3. Think of two or three ethical decisions you made this week and ask yourself, why did I make those decisions? What standard (or universal) does this reflect?

4. Why does the book suggest only two basic points of view for ethics? Do you agree or disagree? Why?

5. Why is the meaning of words important to the discussion of business ethics? Give your definition of business ethics and the worldview that shapes the definition.

6. Define the following terms:
    - worldview   - morals
    - heart   - values
    - ethics

7. Briefly explain Ruddell's model. Think of one or two examples where you (or someone else) had to "find a common ground for doing business"? Was it difficult to maintain your own standards in the process?

8. What does the slogan "business is business" mean? Describe examples of this mindset in your organization (or one where you might be involved in the future).

9. Discuss a way to address those who hold the view that "business is business" and give 10 examples of how ethics is good for business. As an action item, share 2 or 3 (or all 10!) with someone who doubts that ethics has anything to do with business. How did they respond?

10. Review the Train diagram and use it to explain how ethics is important to business strategy. Review your organization's vision and mission statements and see how the ethics statement relates, if at all.

UNDERSTAND YOUR OWN ETHICS

Now THAT WE HAVE LAID out some basic principles, let's shift gears and start addressing the heart of the book, starting with you understanding your own ethics. Let's get personal!

STOP AND THINK

Think about your job. Take your time. Let's reflect. Maybe you work in a corporation, or you own your own small business, or you do contract work for different people. Maybe you pour out sweat every day in a manufacturing plant and it is amazing that you have found time to look at this book! Maybe you work for the government, or you work for a non-profit organization whose cause is very dear to you, or you are a student wrestling with the idea of exactly what you want to do. Think about it.

Now remember the last time you faced a difficult decision. How did you determine what to do? Why did you decide that one action was right and another action was wrong? Perhaps then (as well as now) you find that you don't want to answer the question *why*. You really don't want to think. It is too complicated or maybe you have already heard the issue hashed out with your social network with no conclusion so there is no need for you to really think about it. You just go with what your gut tells you; what feels right. Perhaps, on the other hand, you really do want to do the right thing and you need direction and encouragement to continue in this good path. In either case, you still want to be successful.

It is a challenge, isn't it? On the one hand, deep down you know that there must be standards of right and wrong. On the other hand, you may not have time or energy or maybe even interest to think about them, much less think about how those standards fit in with business success and profitability. You are busy. You have a job to do. You have a business to run. You have a life to live. Yet when you slow down, you realize that you would like to do more. Sometimes you feel like two different people; you act one way at work, and you act differently with family and friends. You think *business is business*. Business requires you to act a certain way in order to compete and succeed. If you have read this far; you are one of the ones who wants to grow, who wants to make their life count, who wants to do and be their best. You figure that you will spend 20 to 30 to 40 or even more years in the work world; much of your life. Don't you think it's worth it to spend a few hours figuring out how you will spend that time? ... to what purpose?

I can remember as a seven-year-old boy in Charlotte, North Carolina lying in bed late at night and thinking about my life. I realized that I would spend time on this earth and then I would pass away. I wondered what death would be like. I thought long and hard about my purpose. What is the point? Why am I here? It has been a long journey to discover some answers, but even from that young age I have made it my aim to seek them.

How about you? Are you purpose-driven? Why do you do what you do, particularly as it applies to that important area of your work; where you spend the majority of your time week in and week out?

This book is about helping you explore what you **believe**, because I am firmly convinced that this is what forms the foundation for the decisions you make in your work. If you do not know what you believe, then your decisions at work will be haphazard at best, destructive for you and others at worst. I think that you will find this exploration very freeing. Once you find out what you really believe and act on that belief, then you will find a unity between the real you outside of work and how you act in your job. It will help you find work situations that are in line with what you believe, not working against what you believe.

It will help others work with you as you understand and articulate to them what you believe. Finally, it may help you realize that you want to change your beliefs to something different!

LET'S BEGIN

I have a deep interest in how belief (faith) and practical life integrate. This has been an age-old issue but perhaps we have ignored or confused this important pursuit in today's world. The idea is that what you believe can affect in an appropriate way all that you do in life. You don't have to make a separation between who you are and what you do day by day at work. There can be a unity; in fact I would argue that in order to be fully true to yourself, there must!

The study of business ethics has many different perspectives. The one I plan to take in this chapter and following is unique. Rather than give general information about a variety of theories and leave it to the reader to determine the veracity of each idea, I will take a more personal case study approach. I will give you my views in detail; you might say a consultant's point of view on the topics. There are benefits to this approach. You will see not only the raw information about business ethics, but also the analysis. So instead of a piece of raw wood, you will see that wood cut, fitted, and stained to perfection to produce a desk. You may not like this particular style of desk, but at least you can use it fully assembled. The idea is that if you can see the process of my thought as well as the content, it can serve as a model for you of how to go about discovering your own belief and integrating that belief with your work.

Another benefit to my approach is that I am letting you know my bias. Many texts present information as neutral, yet the author has a certain perspective (that may be hidden to the reader) that they want to communicate in the book.[1] I think this practice is dishonest. Let's be

---

[1]   It is almost impossible to be totally neutral when writing about any topic. Your bias will determine the issues to discuss and what information is brought forward

open. Let's be clear about what we believe. Let's let the ideas speak for themselves instead of trying to influence through stealth. We should have confidence in what we believe. We should have the willingness to have our ideas (not merely a caricature of them) fully examined and criticized. I think my ideas stand up to scrutiny, so I am more than willing to clearly present them. The hope of this book is that you do the same thing; identify your belief and communicate it to others. It is the ethical thing to do. It is the purposeful thing to do. Let my words encourage you to think about what **you** really believe. So, by the end of the book you will have a well thought out basis for how you carry out your work. You owe it to yourself and those with whom you work to do that! In addition, I guarantee you that in the process you will become a more complete person. You will find that unity between who you really are and how you act at work. You might say that this book could set you free!

Obviously, one negative aspect of the book is that you will not be exposed to all of the arguments surrounding business ethics. My contention is that there are plenty of good books out there that attempt to do just that. They perform an excellent service in helping us understand what people are saying about business ethics. It is useful to look at these books and understand what others think. In order to be effective in business, you have to understand the different people with whom you will do business. However, I think (and others concur) that business ethics is most specifically about the heart. What are you going to do when no one else is around and your business is on the line? What example will you set for others? What ethical standards do you really believe, deep down?

In this book, I do not plan to cover all of the particular ethical issues that you will face in business. I will present some examples, but it is impossible to try to anticipate all of the particular situations that

---

about those issues and what information is withheld. About the closest we can come to *neutrality* is to present differing views on issues and let the proponents of each view speak for themselves. This is very difficult to achieve.

you will face. My desire is that you will think through what you believe so that you begin to build a **foundation** for ethics. Once you have the foundation, then you can apply it to particular situations. Without this firm foundation, discussions about particular ethical issues are meaningless. It is like building a house with beautiful furniture, large rooms, and the most expensive roof; but with no solid slab or wooden beams for a foundation. The house will not hold up when severe weather hits, not to mention the various forms of wild life that might creep up from below!

ETHICS AND LEADERSHIP

This book places a high emphasis on leadership. I think that you should function as a leader in your work environment whether or not you are directly in charge according to the organizational chart. Leaders who are not visible are sometimes called *shadow leaders.* Normally, this refers to leaders who are not readily visible to outside parties. For example, people might remember the players on a great football team, but they forget the coach. The coach is effective, but he is so focused on building his players that people only see the results of his leadership, not him. However, I take the meaning of shadow leadership one step further. I think it refers to the positive influence you can have in an organization whether or not you are directly in charge (noticed or unnoticed). Don't get me wrong. I am not suggesting that you stick your nose into other people's business when you have no right to do so. I am saying that as a shadow leader you are proactive in upholding your own standards and those of the organization. You don't go with the flow. You are your own person. You seek to make a positive difference through your words and actions.

For example, you take a business trip with three other people. During the trip, they discuss how they will pad their expense accounts. As a shadow leader, you are not affected by their actions nor are you legalistic towards your companions. You take the initiative and do what you know is right and through your words and actions encourage your companions to do the same, even to the point of reporting the problem when appropriate. They may or may not follow you, but you are seeking to have an influence. You are displaying leadership qualities in that situation. You are acting as a shadow leader.[2]

One of the problems in business is that no one takes responsibility for ethics in their organizations. We too often go with the flow. Part of the reason for this is ignorance. Sometimes we don't state our opinions because we don't know enough about the business in general or a particular situation to evaluate other people's actions. Sometimes we think (wrongly) that there has to be a conflict between doing business and living ethically. This was true at Global Crossing, a leading edge telecommunications company based in upscale Beverly Hills, California. The company filed bankruptcy on January 28, 2002, the fifth largest bankruptcy case in the history of United States business at the time (Douglass & Rutten, 2002). The company utilized suspect accounting practices, evidently to position themselves in a more positive light against rising competition and to conveniently provide lucrative stock sale options for higher level executives, led by chairman and founder Gary Winnick. Global Crossing used the suspect accounting technique of IRUs (Indefeasible Rights of Use) which allowed them to sell bandwidth on fiber optic network for a long period of time and book their cost over the entire length of the contract, while applying all of the income from the length of the contract to the current year (Douglass & Rutten, 2002). This made the income appear larger for the moment than it really was because it failed to distribute the income over the entire term of the contract. Key executives cashed in on attractive stock sales before a letter written by Roy Olofson, a

---

[2] According to Genesis 1:26, God calls men and women to "... have dominion ..." (ESV) over creation, which also means to be "faithful stewards" and take good care of it. This means, that God has designed us to be leaders. The New Testament highlights this creational leadership role that all of us, especially Christians, should fill: "'You are the light of the world. A city set on a hill cannot be hidden.'" (Matthew 5:14, ESV)

former employee, exposed them (Douglass & Rutten, 2002). Arthur Andersen was their corporate auditor (Murray, 2002). Apparently no one took responsibility for ethical leadership in this situation. Either people did not understand the business well enough to know that unethical activities were taking place, or they failed to act in a timely manner when they saw the wrongs. I want to encourage you through this book to be one who would intervene in a situation like this or in the many other difficult situations you discover at work. Also, I want to encourage you through this book to act in a proactive (and confident) way to develop business ethics in your organization so that problems don't occur in the first place.

WHAT ARE YOUR ETHICS?

This call to leadership begins by you understanding your own standards for ethics and where they come from, the two fundamental business ethics questions. These two questions are important because otherwise the word "ethics" is "just a word." It is interesting to see companies, for example, tout their "ethics" by declaring on their website something like, "our company believes in the highest ethical standards."[3] But this is a meaningless statement. "Highest" based on what? For example, suppose I maintain "high" standards when it comes to high jumping. I crow about my ability to consistently clear 2 feet! Then, someone comes along and says, "by the way, the world record is over 8 feet." After

---

[3] For example, Caterpillar in their ethics handbook called *Our Values in Action* states that they have a commitment "... to maintaining the highest ethical standards ..." (2010) but goes on to explain exactly what that means, which is needed and credible. They also do a good job of understanding how unity and diversity work; "And while our diversity is critical, we also need something to tie us together to operate as one team. Our Code of Conduct doesn't restrict our individuality or give specific instructions to apply in every situation. Instead, the Code serves as a daily reminder of what is expected from every member of the Caterpillar team." (2010)

gasping, I realize that I have just been given a quick lesson in "values clarification."[4]

So, what is your standard for ethics and where does it come from? Begin by listing five or more principles that you stand for. Then write down where those standards come from (getting at your worldview). Do it now!

To provide an example for you, in the next chapter I articulate my standards and where they come from; the Scriptures.[5] This next chapter presents a look at the Biblical standard for ethics as an example. Then the following chapter presents views of others (including potentially the ethics of organizations). Remember that our goal is to clearly understand our own ethics and then discover "a common ground for doing business" in our business situations, so that we keep our own ethics and respect others and their ethical choices (although we may disagree!) and also pursue success (i.e. profit) in our organizations.

---

[4] This is the role of the Law in Scripture. It can't save us, but reminds us of the standard and the realization that we need God's grace and the power of the Holy Spirit in us (through Christ) to do good. See Galatians 3:19, "Why then the law? It was added because of transgressions ..." (ESV). In other words, the Law exposed behavior that might have been seen as "acceptable" (too low a standard) to show that a higher standard was needed.

[5] My view is also summarized by the *Sample Ethics Statement* (see Appendix A).

CHAPTER 2 QUESTIONS FOR REVIEW

1. Think about 2 or 3 times that you faced difficult situations. How did you determine what to do? Why did you decide that one action was right and another action was wrong?
2. Why is it difficult for a book to cover every ethical issue in business? What is an alternative approach?
3. Explain "shadow leadership" and how an understanding of this concept should impact you.
4. Why don't more people do something about business ethics in organizations?
5. List five or more principles that you stand for. Then write down where those standards come from (getting at your worldview).

Chapter 3

UNDERSTAND BIBLICAL BUSINESS ETHICS

NOW THAT YOU HAVE A basic understanding of business ethics definitions, a business ethics model, an appreciation of the importance of business ethics for long-term business success, and have taken a crack at clarifying your own ethics; let's look at how faith (or belief or worldview) integrates with business.

I gave an exam in one of my business ethics classes awhile back that included several essay questions. A part of one of the questions asked the students to give the Christian view of business ethics. One student wrote as part of his answer, "The Christian approach is not different from most of the views that we have discussed in class because I believe all of them encourage people to act ethically." This student underscores the confusion that people have about the meaning of terms and the importance of the definitions that we examined in chapter 1. It is true that all ethical theories encourage people to act ethically, as the student suggests. However, the student missed the essential concept: **What is the standard by which people are to act ethically**? This student does not understand the Christian view or his own point of view. Solutions to ethical issues cannot be true and false at the same time. When the Christian position conflicts with another position, one is true and the other is not. On certain issues, Christianity will differ greatly from other points of view. On other issues it will not. The

Christian foundation to business ethics, however, is different because it is a distinctive worldview.[1]

In this chapter, we will examine how the Christian faith (my worldview) applies to work. I want this chapter to serve as an example of someone who is trying to apply his faith to the work environment in a real way. I hope this will serve as a model of how to put faith and work together even though we may disagree over the faith content.[2]

I appeal to the Scriptures as the standard of faith for the Christian position. I will present an overview of what the Scriptures say about work and business and then give more specific examples. In chapter 5, we will use the Christian faith position to solve particular ethical issues and to establish an ethics program (chapter 6). This material highlights critical areas for you to consider as you continue to develop your own framework for business ethics.

Many times Christians are not willing to believe that their faith holds up in the work environment. They don't think God is big enough to take care of the most challenging situations. As Blamires (1963) points out, "But as a thinking being, the modern Christian has succumbed to secularization. He accepts religion - its morality, its worship, its spiritual culture; but he rejects the religious view of life …" (p. 3). Blamires (1963) goes on to say:

> The mental secularization of Christians means that nowadays we meet only as worshipping beings and as moral beings, not as thinking beings. We agree that it is right to be present on the Lord's own day in the Lord's own house. We agree that it is sinful to commit adultery or to slander our neighbors. But we cannot meet, as thinking Christians, over

---

[1] I am talking about historic Christianity as described in the Apostles' Creed: the literal and historic death and resurrection of Jesus Christ to pay the penalty for our sins, God as creator of the Heavens and Earth out of nothing, and the virgin birth (to name a few). We should also add the Reformed tenet of the perspicuity (clarity and *understandability*) of Scripture (Scripture interprets Scripture).

[2] We will discuss other "faiths" in the next chapter.

the controversial political, social, and cultural issues whose airing constitutes the side of the Church. (p. 16)

Blamires is saying that many people segment their Christianity into a Sunday morning experience. During the week, these same Christians live according to secular standards. Schaeffer (1968) calls this *the fog*; the fact that Christians have adopted secular standards for living without even knowing it.

My stance in this book is quite the opposite. We want to embrace our faith everyday. We know that it is relevant to business ethics. We want to intentionally apply this faith-based reality. Just because some have not applied the faith properly,[3] doesn't mean that it doesn't work. In fact, a real application of a real faith, based on real Truth, will work every time.

Let's examine the Christian view of business ethics which some may call the doctrine of business ethics.[4] We can summarize the Christian view of business ethics as containing five main principles, based on a relationship of covenant and a perspective of trust in God, not money:

1. Have a long term, big picture perspective;
2. Be honest;
3. Be wise;
4. Be diligent;
5. Do good to people.

---

[3] Christians are often too legalistic or too loose. See discussion on *legalism* and *antinomianism* in chapter 5.

[4] Keep in mind that others may, rightly, look to other sections of Scripture as a starting point (i.e. 10 Commandments). However, the Wisdom literature (i.e. Proverbs and Ecclesiastes) is specifically written to "make one wise" (Proverbs 1:2) which includes facing and properly handling sticky situations faced in, for example, business and politics. See the rest of the discussion of Proverbs 1 later in this chapter.

THE COVENANT AS THE FOUNDATION
FOR BUSINESS ETHICS

Before describing the five principles in more detail, we must understand the role of the covenant in Scriptures and its corresponding role in business ethics. The covenant is a deep truth that bridges generations and cultures. Robertson (1987) relates the story of how a tribe of cannibals (the Garlocks) demonstrated their peace with others by cutting the throat of a white bird and sprinkling the blood on both parties. This indicated that they would no longer shed the blood of each other. In other words, they would not eat each other. Robertson (1987) gives this and other examples to show that the covenantal idea is transcultural. Marriage ceremonies of all cultures reflect this covenantal commitment. There are vows and signs of the commitment. Historically, the covenantal format is reflected through international treaties. Pava (2003) concurs that the covenant provides the unifying framework for a number of today's businesses:

> Increasingly, many corporate managers are looking to the covenant model for inspiration, guidance, and most of all, practical business wisdom. ... Though some managers exploit the religiously inspired language of covenant for purely self-interested reasons, other managers and executive - among them Tom Chappell of Tom's of Maine, Max De Pree of Herman Miller, Aaron Feurstein of Malden Mills, and C. William Pollard of ServiceMaster - express an authentic attachment to the idea. ... In fact, one might argue that the seemingly ubiquitous idea of "the stakeholder" descends directly descends directly from the blending of the covenant model and more traditional theory of business. (p. 1)

We will use the covenant as a framework for discussing global business ethics.

Description of the Covenant

In Christianity, God keeps His promise even when the other party (you or I) does not.[5] He sacrifices for the person with whom He has made a covenant, even to the point of death. He does this because He has bound Himself to the terms of the covenant. God promises to deal faithfully with His people in love and in truth. This love puts pressure on people.[6] You cannot escape this relationship. Either you will respond to His love and truth, and comply with His way of doing things, thus making progress in His Kingdom (or company), or you will reject His way of doing things and hold on to your own patterns. However, there are consequences for rejecting His generosity. Either way you must respond to Him because of His intimate interest in you. God is absolutely serious about His covenant commitments. God signified His seriousness initially through the parts and blood of a sacrificed animal and finally through His ultimate sacrifice; the crucifixion and blood of His only Son (represented now in Christian tradition through the bread and wine taken in the Lord's Supper).[7] Other signs for this special relationship were given including a rainbow,[8] circumcision,[9] and the Sabbath.[10]

The covenant is the guiding principle in business ethics because it hits at the heart of business: trusting committed relationships with accountability. As Robertson (1987) asserts, "Responsibilities at work

---

[5] See Romans 5:8 where God loves us despite our rejecting Him, "But God demonstrates His own love toward us, in that while we were still sinners, Christ died for us."

[6] See Romans 12:20-21, "Therefore 'If your enemy is hungry feed him; If he is thirsty, give him a drink; For in so doing you will heap burning coals of fire on his head.' Do not be overcome by evil, but overcome evil with good."

[7] See Genesis 15:10-18 where Abraham cut a heifer, female goat, and ram in two and then God Himself provided the fire to burn the sacrifice as He made His covenant with Abraham. See also Luke 22:20 where Jesus told His disciples, "Likewise He also took the cup after supper, saying, 'This cup is the new covenant in My blood, which is shed for you.'"

[8] See Genesis 9:12-17.

[9] See Genesis 17:9-14.

[10] See Exodus 31:13.

derive meaning only from understanding the bond that God first made with the world at creation" (p. 5). We can see this point dimly reflected by the fact that most business people think relationships are important, but many distort this view by seeing people as targets to manipulate or deceive in order to achieve selfish goals. This might work for the short run, but it is destructive to business in the long run, in a general sense, but also to the deceitful individual.

For example, I was shopping a number of years ago in the market place of a large international city. I was looking for a tie because I had failed to pack one. I went to one place and inquired about the price and was told "$18." I declined and moved on. I subsequently found another place that had the same exact tie for $7. I could understand a discrepancy of a few dollars, but not a $11 difference. The first store certainly had the right to charge $18 for the tie. However, I also had the freedom to not buy from them. Because the second store appeared to consider customers (including me) more in their pricing I will be much more likely to do business with them in the future rather than the first company. We trust business people as customers, vendors, and employers. This is the foundation for business transactions. If I order a certain number of shirts, I expect the vendor to deliver the correct number of shirts at the right time for the right price. If the vendor does not deliver those shirts, then customers cannot buy what they want and the trust for the vendor is broken.

This example goes to the heart of the covenant: **trust**. A covenant is a very sober agreement between a superior (in Biblical times, a suzerainty) and a subordinate (in Biblical times, a vassal). The agreement begins with a preamble highlighting the history of the relationship. It continues with a description of the requirements from the superior. Then it moves to the terms provided for the subordinate. The rewards and punishments are then delineated based on whether or not both parties keep the agreement. The covenant then concludes with some sign or seal. This marks the seriousness of the agreement and serves as a reminder to both parties of the requirements agreed upon. In business, we use contracts, verbal pledges, or Statements of Work (SOWs). All of these are meant to indicate what we pledge to do based on the specifics listed in the agreement.

The Scriptures communicate that we all live in a covenantal relationship with God. In fact, our work particularly reveals this covenantal relationship. Note that several prominent scholars argue, I think successfully, that the book of Deuteronomy is written in the format of an ancient Near Eastern (primarily Hittites who were located in modern day Turkey) treaty or, in our case, a business contract.[11]

Work as Part of the Covenant

Now that we have a basic understanding of the covenant, let's look at some of the verses relating the covenant to **work**. God charges Adam and Eve to rule over the Earth, "Then God blessed them, and God said to them, 'Be fruitful and multiply; fill the earth and subdue it; have dominion over the fish of the sea, over the birds of the air, and over every living thing that moves on the earth.'" (Genesis 1:28) He points out that work, in itself, is not bad; in fact, it is part of who we are, as human beings, made in God's image: "Then the LORD God took the man and put him in the Garden of Eden to tend and to keep it." (Genesis 2:15) However, because of the Fall, work is difficult.[12] Work can also become an object of idolatry: "Then I [King Solomon] looked on all the works that my hands had done and on the labor in which I

---

[11] See Thompson (1974, pp. 14-21) where he cites primarily Mendenhall for the research supporting this idea, but also the original efforts of Gerhard von Rad and, more recently, Meredith Kline. This covenantal approach serves as an interesting model for structuring business contracts. The elements cited by Thompson (1974, pp. 17-18) from Kline include: 1. **Preamble** (who the mediator is of the agreement); 2. **The historical prologue** (description of the history of the relationship; important because relationships are key to the success of the agreement; 3. **The covenant stipulations** (the details of the relationship); 4. **The covenant sanctions** (benefits for keeping stipulations and consequences for ignoring stipulations); 5. **The covenant continuity** (how the covenant will continue).

[12] Genesis 3:17-19

had toiled; and indeed all was vanity and grasping for the wind. There was no profit under the sun."[13] (Ecclesiastes 2:11) (brackets added) So, work is critical to who we are as human beings, but because of the Fall, work is difficult and it can become an idol for us.

It is impossible to look at people apart from the labor they perform. It is insightful that God comments on His original covenant when He describes how He will use Noah's influence to ease people from their labor: "And he called his name Noah, saying, 'This one will comfort us concerning our work and the toil of our hands, because of the ground which the LORD has cursed.'" (Genesis 5:29) This is significant because at this critical juncture of starting over after the destruction of all mankind, God is reasserting his original injunction to mankind to rule and subdue the earth (Genesis 1:28) and work is the means for fulfilling that calling as mankind. Work is tied to the normal everyday activities in which men and women participate as part of God's creation plan: "He appointed the moon for seasons; The sun knows its going down ... Man goes out to his work And to his labor until the evening. O Lord how manifold are Your works! In wisdom You have made them all." (Psalm 104:19-24)

Perhaps the clearest statement of God's plan for work is in the fourth commandment, "Remember the Sabbath, to keep it holy. Six days you shall labor and do all your work but the seventh day is the Sabbath of the Lord." (Exodus 20:8-11) We would not need to rest if we were not working on the other six. God clearly commands; "Six days you shall labor." See how critical this injunction is by noticing how many times

---

[13] See also Ecclesiastes 2 verses 4-10 where Solomon was very busy working hard. The point of these verses is that productive labor was an essential part of Solomon's life, but in the end this productive labor, though laudable, amounted to nothing ultimately because he had the wrong basis for the work. In Ecclesiastes 2:20-23 Solomon realizes that all that he worked so hard for is simply turned over to another; further highlighting the vanity of making labor an end in itself (that which is most important in one's life). As we will see later in this chapter, this is important for business leaders to understand as a starting point for developing business ethics.

it is used in other parts of Scripture.[14] Work is part of His divine plan. It is good. Part of the covenant established with God includes faithful labor. We have special abilities in work: "And I have filled him with the Spirit of God, in wisdom, in understanding, in knowledge, and in all manner of workmanship."[15] (Exodus 31:3, 5, 14, 15) Christ worked as a common laborer.[16] As Robertson (1987) puts it, [even] "Manual labor derives its dignity from this command to subdue the earth" (p. 18). Jesus describes His mission as His work.[17] The connection is important here. Our work at our jobs on earth is a part of our more important work which is to further God's Kingdom. Our work only takes on its proper meaning when we see it in the context of carrying out this greater work. Your business ethics must reflect this context.

---

[14] See Exodus 35:2; Lev 23:3; Numbers 28:25.

[15] These verses describe Bezalel who was called to build the items of the Tabernacle that God had commanded Moses to build. Notice also Exodus 36:1-8 where work is called part of *wisdom* and assumes some kind of *stirring* or calling. See also 1 Chronicles 22:15 where the builders of the temple are called "... skillful men for every kind of work." According to Scripture, work is very important in God's plan for all people.

[16] See Mark 6:3, "'Is this not the carpenter, the Son of Mary, and brother of James, Joses, Judas, and Simon?' ... " Many in the crowd asked this question, thus showing that his labor was common knowledge. Notice that Jesus did not wonder if working as a carpenter was a *good job*. While some may think that not all jobs are important, Jesus our Lord acknowledged that **ALL** labor is worthy, no matter what it is. Paul highlights that no matter what the job, we must do it with enthusiasm knowing that it does make a difference on this earth because the Lord is good and will honor us for what we do for Him: "And whatever you do, do it heartily, as to the Lord and not to men, knowing that from the Lord you will receive the reward of the inheritance for you serve the Lord Christ" (Colossians 3:23, 24).

[17] See John 17:4, "I have glorified You on the earth. I have finished the work which You have given me to do." He accomplished for the Father and all mankind who trust in Him the goal of living a perfect (sinless) life. This allowed Him to serve as the Son of Man, the second Adam who did perfectly keep the Law. This proved Christ's active obedience to the Father and qualified Him to serve as a perfect sacrifice for our sins (see Hebrews 2 and 3, in particular, where this truth is explained in detail). See 2 Corinthians 5:2, "For He made Him who knew no sin to be sin for us, that we might become the righteousness of God in Him."

In summary, work is a blessing. We also realize (Douglas, 1978):

> ... that human [work-related] tasks are given new value and
> become more worth while. They are performed for the sake
> of the name. ... thus [the one who works] is thrice-blessed:
>
> 1. The one who works is blessed in the reception of divine
>   grace to carry through his labors for the glory of God
> 2. Those who receive the results of such tasks done in a new
>   spirit and with a new quality are benefited also
> 3. God is glorified. (pp. 1337 – 1338) (brackets added)

See also Exodus 35-36 where gifted artisans used their work talents to bring glory to God. Paul took pride in working with his own hands.[18] This was in direct contrast with previous views of labor that saw it as a demeaning necessity.[19] Work is part of normal day-to-day life even after conversion. Paul says, "But as God has distributed to each one, as the Lord has called each one, so let him walk." (1 Corinthians 7:17) First Corinthians 7:17-24 assumes people will not change their work (and other aspects of their situation) upon conversion. Paul worked as a tent maker to support himself, even while in ministry.[20] This was his

---

[18] See in 1 Corinthians 4:12, "And we labor, working with our own hands. Being reviled, we bless; being persecuted, we endure."

[19] See Cavanagh (1998, pp. 108-110) on ancient Greek views towards work, "The ancient Greeks thought of work and commerce as demeaning to a citizen. At best, it was a burden required for survival" (p. 108).

[20] See Acts 18:3, "So, because he was of the same trade, he stayed with them and worked; for by occupation they were tentmakers."

occupation. Paul provided for himself and others.[21] Work is an integral part of who we are, no matter what our spiritual status.[22]

Because work is part of God's fundamental covenantal plan for us, our attitude while working must reflect our awareness of that plan. This means that we strive to do our very best, knowing that our work is for the Lord. We work directly for Him. This means that we draw strength from Him to work and we want our work to be great in order to please Him. God is creative in His work. We want to reflect that creativity in how we perform our work, no matter how (seemingly) mundane the job or how difficult the boss. In God's covenantal economy, every job has meaning because He is pleased with the one who works hard with a good attitude. God receives this hard work as an offer of praise. This wonderful dynamic is summed up in Colossians 3:23, "And whatever you do, do it heartily, as to the Lord and not to men."[23]

---

[21] See Acts 20:34, "Yes, you yourselves know that these hands have provided for my necessities and for those who were with me. I have shown you in every way, by laboring like this, that you must support the weak. And remember the words of the Lord Jesus, that He said, 'It is more blessed to give than to receive.'"

[22] See also 1 Timothy 5:8, "But if anyone does not provide for his own, and especially for those of his household, he has denied the faith and is worse than an unbeliever." Notice the critical role of labor as the means for providing basic needs (food and clothing) for one's family.

[23] This passage is penned in the midst of instructions to *bondservants* (employees) on how they should work for their bosses. Do not miss the point. You work hard for your boss because you are not really working for the boss, but for the Lord. This is freeing but it also holds you responsible. The idea is that you work with enthusiasm (*heartily*) like you mean it, not just doing the minimum at the times when the boss is looking. See also Ephesians 6:5-6, "Bondservants, be obedient to those who are your masters according to the flesh, with fear and trembling, in sincerity of heart, as to Christ; not with eyeservice, as men-pleasers, but as bondservants of Christ, doing the will of God from the heart." Notice too the contrast in motive between the Christian (working for an eternal and just God) versus Secularists (working for temporary selfish pursuits) versus Marxists (working for the man-made State). Christianity properly blends freedom and responsibility.

Let's look at one more important principle before we look at the particulars of what the scriptures teach on business ethics. This is the principle that work and making money (in and of themselves) are ultimately meaningless. This is a simple, yet powerful truth that forms the critical perspective from which we build our covenantal foundation of business ethics. This truth emerges in a profound way in the book of Ecclesiastes.

GAINING A BUSINESS ETHICS
PERSPECTIVE - ECCLESIASTES

To understand the scriptural point of view regarding business ethics, we have to look closely at the book of Ecclesiastes. The book of Ecclesiastes is critical because its theme is that of purpose by one who had it all and because he had it all, he could speak with utmost experience about what life really means. Many of us dream of what life would be like if we only had more. Solomon had more and then some, yet he stated clearly that the more, and then some from this world wasn't enough ... **PERIOD**. Ecclesiastes, being Wisdom literature, tries to help us learn from another's experience. He evaluates human experience from every sought after value: knowledge, sexual experience, wealth and its accouterments, beauty, respect of others, power, total self-expression and fulfillment and says it all comes up short. You might say that he takes aim at all major secular philosophical systems and finds them wanting: knowledge (Gnosticism), sexual experience and sensuality (hedonism), pure self indulgence (Rousseau and the drug culture), wealth and its accouterments (raw capitalism and pragmatism), beauty and emotionalism (romanticism), respect of others (psychological theories), power (nihilism), and self-fulfillment (existentialism). Ecclesiastes is like a Woody Allen film but with a very different conclusion. Yes, Solomon realizes (like Allen) that despite all earthly successes, you cannot cheat death; a fact that other views dismiss. That is the cold, hard fact. So, in his thinking he is forced to look at purpose: how do we find meaning in this life knowing that death is inevitable?[24]

It hits at the foundation of business ethics because it tells us about a purpose which supersedes all others. It asks the question: do hard work, success, and GREAT wealth lead to fulfillment (in and of themselves)? And the answer is resoundingly NO! Ecclesiastes is perhaps the most real book in the Bible. This is your reality check as you think about developing your business ethics standards.

As Kidner (1976) puts it:

> The function of Ecclesiastics is to bring us to the point where we begin to fear that such a comment is the only honest one. So it is, if everything is dying. We face the appalling inference that nothing has meaning, nothing matters under the sun. It is then that we can hear, as the good news which it is, that everything matters – "for God will bring every deed into judgment, with every secret thing, whether good or evil." (p. 18)

Kidner (1976) points out the abuse of leadership that we see in Ecclesiastes:

> … the envy that inspires, or else attends success (4:14); the money-fixation that makes the lonely tycoon a pathetic and pointless figure (4:7, 8); the vanity that sustains a fool too long in office (4:13), … But chiefly he mourns "the oppressions that are practiced under the sun" (4:1). … The well-organized man may bask in self-sufficiency, but Qoheleth sees through it. It is self-deception. Even the most limited and predictable prizes in life - let alone the quest for

---

[24] "Whatever my eyes desired I did not keep from them. I did not withhold my heart from any pleasure, For my heart rejoiced in all my labor; And this was my reward from all my labor. Then I looked on all the works that my hands had done And on the labor in which I had toiled; And indeed all was vanity and grasping for the wind." (Ecclesiastes 2:10-11).

something ultimate - can go astray, and a man be left with nothing (Ecclesiastes 9:12). (p. 18)

As Kidner (1976) summarizes the purpose, the writer of Ecclesiastes is "demolishing to build" (p. 19).

This is why Ecclesiastes establishes the Christian business ethics perspective. The author presents every secular reason for pursuing business and then refutes it through further analysis.[25] Ecclesiastes 3:11 summarizes: "He has made everything beautiful in its time. Also He has put eternity in their hearts, except that no one can find out the work that God does from beginning to end." There are things we value on Earth, but nothing that endures because we lose any ability to have an impact (such as making money) when we die. "That is how the book will end. On this rock [of vain pursuits of business and other endeavors] we can be destroyed: but it is rock, not quicksand. There is the chance to build" (Kidner, 1976, p. 19) (brackets added).

Now let us look at some of the particular statements the writer of Ecclesiastes makes about the meaning of work and the wealth it produces.

Ecclesiastes on Purpose

Ecclesiastes 1:3 - "What profit has a man from all his labor in which he toils under the sun?" The word "profit" used here is used as a business word; so it is almost as if the author is using a play on words. He might be saying something like this: "you are making money in your labor, but where is it getting you ultimately"?

---

[25] Kidner (1976) suggests that the author of Ecclesiastes is using, "the Mesopotamian dialogue between master and servant: ... when you learn to laugh at everything you are soon left with nothing worth the bother of a laugh. Triviality is more stifling than tragedy, and the shrug is the most hopeless of all comments on life" (p. 19).

Ecclesiastes 3:9-10 - "What profit has the worker from that in which he labors? I have seen the God-given task with which the sons of men are to be occupied." With the perspective of wisdom gained through experience, the writer realizes that there is no ultimate profit to be gained from labor. He knows. He has seen the task (labor as defined in Genesis 3 as part of subduing the earth).

Ecclesiastes 5:12-17

> The sleep of a laboring man is sweet, Whether he eats little or much; But the abundance of the rich will not permit him to sleep. There is a severe evil which I have seen under the sun: Riches kept for their owner to his hurt. But those riches perish through misfortune; When he begets a son, there is nothing in his hand. As he came from his mother's womb, naked shall he return, To go as he came; And he shall take nothing from his labor Which he may carry away in his hand. And this also is a severe evil - Just exactly as he came, so shall he go. And what profit has he who has labored for the wind? All his days he also eats in darkness, And he has much sorrow and sickness and anger.

This passage is perhaps the most pointed in describing the personal prison in which the greedy man lives. He thinks that he is powerful and in control, but deep down, if he stops to think (which is rare, if at all), he knows that another day brings the shrill voice of his taskmaster; greed. Contrast this with the peaceful sleep of one who works hard, enjoys the fruit of his labor (whatever it is), but does not covet. Which way do you choose to live?

Ecclesiastes on Satisfaction

Ecclesiastes 1:8 - "All things are full of labor; Man cannot express it. The eye is not satisfied with seeing, Nor the ear filled with hearing." We see here that even though we labor, we are not satisfied in labor itself.

Ecclesiastes 2:18-23

> Then I hated all my labor in which I had toiled under the
> sun, because I must leave it to the man who will come
> after me. And who knows whether he will be wise or a
> fool? Yet he will rule over all my labor in which I toiled
> and in which I have shown myself wise under the sun. This
> also is vanity. Therefore I turned my heart and despaired
> of all the labor in which I had toiled under the sun. For
> there is a man whose labor is with wisdom, knowledge,
> and skill; yet he must leave his heritage to a man who has
> not labored for it. This also is vanity and a great evil. For
> what has man for all his labor, and for the striving of his
> heart with which he has toiled under the sun? For all his
> days are sorrowful, and his work burdensome; even in the
> night his heart takes no rest. This also is vanity. Nothing
> is better for a man than that he should eat and drink, and
> that his soul should enjoy good in his labor. This also, I
> saw, was from the hand of God.

This long passage sums it up; you cannot take it with you. As someone
put it, you do not find a moving truck behind a hearse. Other people
take our things when we die and often misuse them. We see that the
goal is to enjoy work[26] ("nothing is better"); but at times it is difficult
because deep down, we know that we can lose the fruits of our labor.

---

[26] Even if you enjoy your work, you may not be laboring to please God. People can
behave *ethically* in business and still not be Believers. However, I would argue
that they are acting this way for one of several reasons; because of some Christian
heritage (in the form of behavior patterns) that has been passed on to them but
they do not acknowledge God for the positive patterns they possess (they are
receiving benefits of Christian heritage but not thanking God as the source of
this blessing), they pragmatically act out Christian business values because they
work (the premise of this book), or they are under constraints because of the
organizational culture and when put under enough pressure will show their true
nature and act unethically.

Ecclesiastes 4:8-10

> There is one alone, without companion: He has neither son
> nor brother. Yet there is no end to all his labors, Nor is his
> eye satisfied with riches. But he never asks, "For whom do
> I toil and deprive myself of good?" This also is vanity and
> a grave misfortune. Two are better than one, Because they
> have a good reward for their labor. For if they fall, one will
> lift up his companion. But woe to him who is alone when
> he falls, For he has no one to help him up.

This is a vivid picture of one who has joined the "rat race" to the point
of ignoring his family. The key phrase is "Nor is his eye satisfied with
riches." As Kidner (1976) puts it: "Such a man, even with a wife and
children, will have little time for them, convinced that he is toiling for
their benefit although his heart is elsewhere, devoted and wedded to
his projects" (pp. 46-47).

Ecclesiastes 6:7-8 - "All the labor of man is for his mouth, And
yet the soul is not satisfied. For what more has the wise man than the
fool? What does the poor man have, Who knows how to walk before
the living?"

Ecclesiastes 5:18-19

> Here is what I have seen: It is good and fitting for one to eat
> and drink, and to enjoy the good of all his labor in which he
> toils under the sun all the days of his life which God gives
> him; for it is his heritage. As for every man to whom God
> has given riches and wealth, and given him power to eat of
> it, to receive his heritage and rejoice in his labor - this is the
> gift of God.

Ecclesiastes 3:12-13 - "I know that nothing is better for them than to
rejoice, and to do good in their lives, and also that every man should
eat and drink and enjoy the good of all his labor - it is the gift of God."

Notice here that it is NOT inherently wrong to enjoy what you earn from your labor. It is all a matter of perspective.

In summarizing our key business ethics perspective from Ecclesiastes, let us take a look at I Timothy 6.

I TIMOTHY 6 AND THE ROLE OF WEALTH

This chapter is perhaps the clearest statement in Scriptures about the proper perspective towards money and business ethics. It summarizes everything that Ecclesiastes has been telling us and applies it realistically. Let's look at the passage in detail.

I Timothy is called a Pastoral epistle. Timothy was a convert from a Jewish mother and Greek father near modern day Konya in Turkey.[27] In it Paul counsels the young pastor,[28] Timothy, about how to run the church[29] and particularly how to deal with the different types of people that he will encounter. It is precisely in this practical Christian guidebook that Paul talks about the essential business topics of workers, money, and what to do about wealth.

Paul begins chapter 6 with instructions to *bondservants* (slaves). In the Roman Empire, you could call most of the blue-collar working class

---

[27] See Acts 16:1, "Then he [Paul] came to Derbe and Lystra and behold, a certain disciple was there, named Timothy, the son of a certain Jewish woman who believed, but his father was Greek." (brackets added)

[28] Paul calls him a "son" in the faith (I Timothy 1:2). See also I Timothy 4:12 where Paul says, "Let no one despise your youth, but be an example to the believers." Evidently people were looking down on Timothy and not taking him seriously precisely because he was young. Notice Paul's emphasis on setting an example in leadership.

[29] Timothy traveled extensively with Paul (see Acts 17:14-15; 18:5; 19:22; 20:4 and Romans 16:20). However, he was appointed to pastor the church in Corinth, a very difficult group. See I Corinthians 4:17, "For this reason I have sent Timothy to you, who is my beloved and faithful son in the Lord, who will remind you of my ways in Christ, as I teach everywhere in every church." It appears Timothy also served (probably briefly) in Philippi. See Philippians 2:19, "But I trust in the Lord Jesus to send Timothy to you shortly, that I also may be encouraged when I know your state. For I have no one like-minded, who will sincerely care for your state."

bondservants; either through capture, purchase, or to pay off a debt. This category might even include professional workers such as doctors (even though they had special skills, they were still slaves). Paul's instructions to bondservants would apply to employees in today's culture.[30] Paul tells workers to honor their employers (*masters*). This does not mean that workers are passive or do everything that the employer suggests when it involves a personal ethical matter[31], but the goal is to glorify God through this attitude of honor.[32] Even if the employer is difficult, this positive attitude will put pressure on the employer to do the right thing.[33]

Paul emphasizes a special point that if you are a Believer, you must also work hard with a good attitude for your believing boss.[34] Because,

---

[30] In making this parallel between *bondservant* and modern day worker, it is insightful that even in this worst of situations (you actually were a slave instead of like today, when sometimes it just seems that way), Paul encourages faithful work.

[31] See Daniel 1:8-16 where Daniel appealed to his *boss* to not eat the rich foods of the court. In this situation Daniel recommended an alternative ("let me eat vegetables"). Also, Daniel kept in mind the performance goals of his *boss*, which were to look fit for the King's service, and agreed to undergo the quality control determined by the boss. Often religious people want to pursue the requirements of their faith (like days off) but are not willing to consider the performance requirements of their employers. This is not a biblical attitude. The idea is to achieve both.

[32] See I Timothy 6:1b, "... so that the name of God and His doctrine may not be blasphemed." This attitude must also be sincere and backed up by actions. See Ephesians 6:6 where workers are reminded that they must obey "... not with eyeservice, as men-pleasers, but as bondservants of Christ, doing the will of God from the heart, with goodwill doing service, as to the Lord, and not to men." This is the Christian stance; if you have trusted Christ and received the Holy Spirit, you are a new and totally free person on the inside, no matter what your outward circumstances. So Paul encourages workers to understand their internal freedom and willingly serve their masters only because of their love for the Lord, without expectation from the earthly master. This is freedom. The confidence is that in the long run, you will have an influence on those around you (see 1 Corinthians 15:58). This is power.

[33] See Romans 12:21, "Do not be overcome by evil, but overcome evil with good." Also, the Scripture teaches that bosses must behave respectfully towards employees. See Colossians 4:1, "Masters, give your bondservants what is just and fair, knowing that you also have a Master in heaven."

[34] See I Timothy 6:2, "And those who have believing masters, let them not despise them because they are brethren, but rather serve them."

unfortunately, believing employees have the tendency to take their believing bosses for granted and take advantage of them.

Let's look at the heart of the passage that ties it to our theme from Ecclesiastes. Ambition to earn is fine but it must be tempered by a true understanding of contentment. We can say that the strong horse of ambition must be place under the bit of contentment. In I Timothy 6:6, Paul tells us, "Now godliness with contentment is great gain." This is a critical statement because it prefaces everything else that Paul says about money. His emphasis is on **contentment**, being thankful for what you have and OK with what you do not have. Paul concludes this statement by saying that this is the **real gain**.[35] It is not money. The real gain is doing the right thing (what God requires = godliness) with contentment (at peace with the results whether it means you have money and possessions or not). Now listen to his reasoning (as echoed by the writer of Ecclesiastes) in I Timothy 6:7, "For we brought nothing into this world, and it is certain we can carry nothing out."[36] Sound familiar? Here is the argument yet one more time; death is inevitable. We cannot take anything from this world with us when we die. So, in an ultimate

---

[35] Some members of the early church thought that Christianity was a way to gain wealth. It is interesting that some people still look at church this way, as an opportunity to secure customers for their businesses. I was traveling in Eastern Europe a number of years ago and one of my eastern European friends was avoiding another member of the church because the woman was always trying to recruit my friend for her home business. Ward (1974) states, "*Gain* is here a 'means of getting.' The English word is used elsewhere in the sense of 'business.' A slave girl with a spirit of divination was exploited by her masters and brought with them 'much business,' and the hope of yet more of it 'went out' with the spirit which Paul ordered to 'go out' (Acts 16:16, 19). The English *gain* may be used as the opposite of 'loss.' 'Whatever gain I had, I counted as loss for the sake of Christ' (Philippians 3:7). Or it may be used to express an advance on what hitherto had seemed the supreme good: '... to live is Christ, and to die is gain' (Philippians 1:21). It speaks of profit, advantage, of what is helpful or better. 'I must boast; there is nothing to be gained by it ...' (2 Corinthians 12:1)" (p. 96).

[36] Notice the emphasis in this passage, "it is certain." There is absolutely no doubt about death and the fact that we *can't take it with us*. It is (as we discovered in Ecclesiastes) absolutely foolish to think otherwise.

sense, it really doesn't matter what we have or don't have on this earth. God calls us to have contentment either way.

Paul follows with a sobering statement about the basis of our contentment. In other words, **bottom line**, what do we really need? He simply says (I Timothy 6:8), "And having food and clothing, with these we shall be content." **Wow!** That's it. This is all that we really need. Now, clothing in the Greek can have a broader meaning, which includes shelter or protection from the elements. But, it is a pretty simple list isn't it? It is not necessarily wrong to have more than just food or shelter. The important question is: what is the basis for your contentment? "But those who desire to be rich fall into temptation and a snare, and into many foolish and harmful lusts which drown men in destruction and perdition" (I Timothy 6:9). You are a fool if you think that gaining riches will give you happiness and contentment. Those views will harm you in the life to come, if not in this life as well. Paul sums it up, "For the love of money is a root of all kinds of evil, for which some have strayed from the faith in their greediness, and pierced themselves through with many sorrows" (I Timothy 6:10). The word *pierced* has the meaning of taking a spear and thrusting it through your chest. The idea is that you are *killing* yourself by having this lust for money. As Hendricksen (1957) says, "The person who craves riches generally also yearns for honor, popularity, power, ease, and the satisfaction of the desires of the flesh. All spring from the same root, selfishness, which being the worst possible way of *really* satisfying the 'self,' is both senseless and hurtful. So the 'gain' is loss"[37] (p. 200) (emphasis added). You are a fool because the allure of wealth is so powerful, yet it is the worst form of deception. When you find it, nothing is there. It is like eating cotton candy. It is big and fluffy, but when you bite it, it dissolves to nothing. As Hendricksen (1957) says: "The desire to meet the needs of the body is not criticized. It is the yearning for *material riches*, as if these could satisfy the soul, that is here condemned" (p. 199) (emphasis added). Again, riches in and of themselves are not wrong, but if sought after for happiness,

---

[37] Contrast with Matthew 20:26-28 where Jesus says "… whoever desires to become great among you, let him be your servant."

will lead to a dead end and result in misery and distraction from the real issue, our need for peace and contentment in Jesus Christ alone.

Some Christians read these passages and think that money is bad, so it is admirable to be poor. This is the notion of the Pharisees, adding to the Law so they would not break it. But listen carefully to what the Word is saying and not saying. It is saying that to crave riches is wrong ... because it is just stupid (foolish) and leads to more problems than it is worth. However, the passage does NOT say that having a great deal of money is wrong. Given the right attitude, God may choose to bless certain people with wealth for the benefit of others and His Kingdom.

We see in our passage that having money, in itself, is not wrong, because Paul gives instruction to those who do have money. And his instruction is not to chide them for having it, "Command those who are rich in this present age not to be haughty, nor to trust in uncertain riches but in the living God, who gives us richly all things to enjoy" (I Timothy 6:17). So, it is all about our attitude and priorities. Doing good with our riches is what counts,[38] not seeking them as if they will make life work for us. So, let me encourage you; if you strongly desire money instead of ethical conduct with contentment you are (as someone put it), "keeping your eye on the scoreboard, not the ball."[39]

PHILIPPIANS 4:10-13 AND THE SECRET OF CONTENTMENT

Paul sums it up best in Philippians 4:10-13,

> Not that I speak in regard to need, for I have learned in whatever state I am, to be content. I know how to be abased,

---

[38] See 1 Timothy 6:18, "Let them do good, that they be rich in good works, ready to give, willing to share."

[39] The actual quote is (Blanchard, 1988), "Focusing on profit is like keeping your eye on the scoreboard and not on the ball" (p. 107). The meaning of the quote is basically the same as I have used it. Blanchard takes it from the company side (*profit*) where I take it from the personal, ethical side (*desiring money*).

and I know how to abound. Everywhere and in all things
I have learned both to be full and to be hungry, both to
abound and to suffer need.

Paul sends this letter to thank the Philippians for the gift that they so
thoughtfully sent him.[40] As Barclay (1959) points out, Paul uses an
important word from pagan Greek ethics of his day when he talks about
contentment: *autarkeia.* Barclay's (1959) comments are insightful:

> He says that he had learned to be ... *entirely self-sufficient.*
> This *autarkeia*, this self-sufficiency was the highest aim of
> Stoic ethics. By *autarkeia* the Stoics meant a state of mind
> in which a man was absolutely and entirely independent
> of all things and of all people, a state in which a man had
> taught himself to need nothing and to need no one. ... In
> order to achieve contentment the Stoic abolished all desires
> and eliminated all emotions. Love was rooted out of life,
> and caring was forbidden. ... We see at once the difference
> between the Stoics and Paul. The Stoic said, "I will learn
> contentment by a deliberate act of my own will." Paul
> said, "I can do all things through Christ who infuses His
> strength into me." For the Stoic contentment was a human
> achievement; for Paul it was a divine gift. The Stoic was
> *self-sufficient*; but Paul was *God-sufficient.* Stoicism failed
> because it was inhuman; Christianity succeeded because
> it was rooted in the divine. Paul could face anything;[41] he

---

[40] See Philippians 4:15-18, "Now you Philippians know also that in the beginning
of the gospel, when I departed from Macedonia, no church shared with me
concerning giving and receiving but you only. For even in Thessalonica you sent
aid once and again for my necessities. Not that I seek the gift, but I seek the fruit
that bounds to your account. Indeed I have all things sent from you, a sweet-
smelling aroma, an acceptable sacrifice, well pleasing to God."

[41] See his vivid description of exactly what he did face in 2 Corinthians 11:23-31;
including whippings (five), beatings (three), a stoning, shipwrecks (three), robbers,

could have nothing and he could have all things; it made
no difference, because, in any situation he had Jesus Christ.
The man who walks with Christ and lives in Christ can cope
with anything. (pp. 103-105)

This section is critical for helping you form your basic business perspective. If you miss the point concerning contentment, all of the other particulars will mean nothing. If deep down in your heart, you lust after money as the most important thing in life, you will have no success in building a Christian business ethic. Your ethic is at best secular (and hedonistic) and at worst nihilistic. Please hear the many words from Ecclesiastes (and other parts of the Scriptures). Trust the wisdom of this one (Solomon) who has experienced what you crave first hand. **IT DOESN'T WORK!** Money and the things it can buy are not the answers to the life to come or even life on this earth. On the other hand, the Biblical writers are telling you not to be afraid of money either. Money is important in the Scriptures. In fact the accumulation and use of money are powerful indicators of your heart. Where is your heart? Do you have a proper attitude towards money? I am convinced that you can work aggressively to build a successful business (which includes making a profit) and still have the proper attitude towards life.[42] Let's now look at the particulars of making this happen.

FIVE MAIN PRINCIPLES

Now that we have looked at a basic overview of the covenantal approach and its view of work, and taken a look at our foundational attitude in

---

bad weather, sleepless nights, and many difficulties with people (among others).

[42] See Collins' and Porras' (2002) book *Built to Last* on the tyranny of the *or*. They argue that businesses often contrast functions that they should not, like saying *we can make money* **OR** *we can do good to others*; but we can't do both. Collins and Porras argue that great businesses do exactly that. You can make money **AND** do good. They are tightly related. This is the whole point of Chappell's (1999) book *Upside Down*.

business ethics, let's look in more detail at what the Scriptures teach specifically about business ethics. We will concentrate our analysis mainly on the book of Proverbs because this book is meant to give wise advice about all aspects of life. So, we find a great deal of information packed in short, pithy statements in these 31 chapters. In Proverbs, we see patterns of verses pertinent to business clustered around our five main principles. We have already summarized the five basic principles in the first part of this chapter. Now, let's look at the justification for these five principles.

Main Principle #1: Have A Long Term, Big Picture Perspective

One of the primary teachings in the New Testament concerns the Kingdom of God and what that means for Believers. One important aspect of the Kingdom is the relationship between the already (we **already** experience some of His blessing right now on Earth) and the not yet (we have **not yet** tasted the full wondrous joy which we will know in Heaven). It is important for each of us to live right now and give glory to God who has blessed us right now. We see this blessing in several ways: the beautiful creation that we can still enjoy,[43] the fact that evil is bound[44] so people can still be ethical to some degree, and the relationships that

---

[43] See Romans 1:20 where the emphasis is on "since the creation of the world" … insinuating that we can see God's hand in the intricacy and beauty of His creation. See also Genesis 1:31 where everything that God created was *good*.

[44] See Matthew 12:29 where Jesus points out that the one (Jesus Christ) must first bind the "strong man" (Satan) so that he can "plunder his goods" (set captives free). So, even though evil remains, things are not as bad as they could be because the Holy Spirit restrains evil ("binds" it) enough so that the Gospel can have an impact on people (see Philippians 2:15 where God's people are said to "shine" amidst a "perverse and crooked generation"). Also in certain cultures, remnants of a Christian influence remain in children, even though the original Christians are long gone. They have passed on their character qualities to their generations which results in good (see Exodus 3:7 where God shows "mercy for thousands." Of course the reverse, unfortunately, is also true where fathers pass on bad habits to children "to the third and the fourth generation").

we can form.[45] God's people also taste it (experience to some small degree what Heaven will be like) through worship, fellowship, and service. However, the Kingdom of God points to something that is also in the future. This is the rule of God, for all eternity, in Heaven; something to be enjoyed richly by His people.[46] We need to consider this long-term perspective. What we do right now counts for eternity.

This is essential to business ethics. We don't want to sacrifice our long-term success for an unethical, immediate deal. What we fail to consider is that the unethical deal has ramifications for future business; it can harm business in the long run.

You can easily misunderstand this relationship between the already and the not yet. Some focus so much on the future (the not yet) that they are not involved in today. As has been said they "are so heavenly minded that they are no earthly good" (see Niebuhr's *Christ above culture* category in chapter 4). It is important to work hard today.[47]

Proverbs has many verses that highlight this long-term perspective. I will mention six of them.[48]

---

[45] See Genesis 2:18 where He highlights the fundamental desire of all human beings for companionship when He says, "it is not good that man should be alone." This companionship is something we all enjoy.

[46] See Romans 8:16 ff. where Paul reminds us of the purpose behind the difficulties we face in this life (v. 18), "For I consider that the sufferings of this present time [the *already*] are not worthy to be compared with the glory [the *not yet* but something that will happen for certain] which shall be revealed in us." (brackets added)

[47] Live *existentially*. I think this is a useful point that the existentialists make. We need to live in a genuine manner ... **right now**, not distracted by regrets about the past or fears about the future. That is why, for Christians, the work of the Holy Spirit is so important. Only when the Holy Spirit gives you a new heart through belief in Jesus Christ (2 Corinthian 5:17) can you (really you) genuinely live ethically. Without this work of the Spirit, you can try to act ethically but this is not really *you*. That is one of the reasons why the Pharisees (the religious leaders of Jesus' day) came across as hypocritical (*lacking authority*). Obviously, another reason was that the Pharisees **were** hypocrites, doing what they were condemning either overtly or mentally. People can act ethically outwardly, but this outward conformity does not count for eternity.

[48] See also Proverbs 11:21; 11:28; 12:3; 12:12; 12:21; 13:7; 13:19; 13:5; 15:16; 18:12; 19:1; 20:17, 23; 21:17; 23:4, 5; 23:17-18; 24:19-20.

Proverbs 13:11 - "Wealth gained by dishonesty will be diminished, But he who gathers by labor will increase." In the long run, those who gain wealth by persistent (and wise) labor will last, while those who try to take a short cut to wealth will lose out. They may gain wealth in the short run, but they will eventually lose it. Several years ago, I heard about an investment banker named Ahmed who worked as a partner with three other men. Their business did very well for the first two years. Then the three partners decided to use questionable tactics to increase their earnings. When they presented their ideas to Ahmed, he immediately told them that their tactics were unethical and he could not work in an unethical situation. He then sold his share of the business to them and resigned. Fifteen months later, the three men were in prison and the business was ruined. Ahmed went on to secure a great position in a small bank and did well.

Proverbs 14:8 - "The wisdom of the prudent is to understand his way, But the folly of fools is deceit." The application of this passage is interesting. It says that the wise leader learns from his situation. He constantly analyzes and evaluates with the understanding that he will make adjustments. He adapts to markets and customers and develops products that continue to meet needs and these prudent actions lead to long term success. The fool, on the other hand, does not adjust. He does not grow. He continues to produce the same thing but tries to make customers think that they are getting something great.[49] In other words, the fool tries deceit (style over substance) to maintain sales instead of innovation and qualitative growth. This is *folly*.

Proverbs 21:5, 6 - "The plans of the diligent lead surely to plenty, But those of everyone who is hasty, surely to poverty. Getting treasures by a lying tongue is the fleeting fantasy of those who seek death." The one who wants to take short cuts (often by lying) may make money today but it won't last. It will eventually or *surely* lead to poverty. It might take awhile, but short cuts are bad for business. In contrast, the

---

[49] Making the same thing is not necessarily foolish, nor is intense marketing. The fool deceives by misrepresenting his product or making something that violates brand laws (like selling knock-offs).

diligent leader who continues to plan and execute those plans built on an honest foundation will eventually or *surely* lead to plenty.

Proverbs 25:26 - "A righteous man who falters before the wicked is like a murky spring and a polluted well." This verse highlights the tragedy of one who is righteous but who under pressure does not do the right thing. They *falter* (or back off) from doing what they know is right because of the moment. Unfortunately, if this is the case for all the righteous people in an organization, the organization will suffer.

Proverbs 28:20, 22 - "A faithful man will abound with blessings, But he who hastens to be rich will not go unpunished … A man with an evil eye hastens after riches, And he does not consider that poverty will come upon him." Again, the one who desires money **NOW**, no matter what the means, will end up in poverty in the long run. The contrast is also true; the ethical or wise leader will end up successful in the long run.

Finally, we see a pattern in Proverbs where integrity is always regarded as more beneficial than wealth or success gained through dishonest means. Proverbs 16:8 is one example, "Better is a little with righteousness, Than vast revenues without justice."

Main Principle #2: Be Honest

Christianity has a high concern for honesty and the truth. Jesus Christ himself said that he was "the way, *the truth*, and the life."[50] (emphasis added) Paul set an example as an honest laborer.[51] Here are some verses in Proverbs on honesty.[52]

---

[50] John 14:6, "Jesus said to him, 'I am the way, the truth, and the life. No one comes to the Father except through Me.'"

[51] See Acts 18:3, "So, because he was of the same trade, he stayed with them and worked; for by occupation they were tentmakers." See also 2 Thessalonians 3:8, "… nor did we eat anyone's bread free of charge, but worked with labor and toil night and day, that we might not be a burden to any of you, not because we do not have authority, but to make ourselves an example of how you should follow us." Notice how he modeled honest labor even amidst a busy ministry.

[52] Others include: Proverbs 4:14; 4:19; 6:17; 6:12-15; 12:22; 13:5; 16:11, 13; 17:23; 19:5, 9; 20:10; 28:13.

Proverbs 4:24 - "Put away from you a deceitful mouth, And put perverse lips far from you." We must not speak in a deliberately deceitful way to those who deserve the truth, whether on a personal or business level.

Proverbs 6:16, 19 - "These six things the Lord hates ... A false witness who speaks lies, And one who sows discord among brethren." There is a relationship between lying and *discord* (conflict) among people in groups. Discord is a big problem in organizations because it stifles productivity (having to spend time and effort to resolve the conflict rather than investing that same time and effort in productivity) and creates a negative environment for workers. If you experience discord in your organization, perhaps it is because people (normally leaders) are habitually lying when carrying out their business.

Proverbs 8:6-9

> Listen, for I will speak of excellent things, And from the opening of my lips will come right things; For my mouth will speak truth; Wickedness is an abomination to my lips. All the words of my mouth are with righteousness; Nothing crooked or perverse is in them. They are all plain to him who understands, And right to those who find knowledge.

This passage emphasizes the importance of speaking truth ("excellent things"). The hearer who is honest will clearly understand what another honest person ("those who find knowledge") says. The application is that if someone does not understand or thinks foolishly about what an honest person says, perhaps they are "crooked or perverse."[53]

Proverbs 10:19-21 - "In the multitude of words sin is not lacking But he who restrains his lips is wise. The tongue of the righteous is choice silver; The heart of the wicked is worth little. The lips of the

---

[53] Obviously, in business two people can have a misunderstanding due to communication problems. You should first address that possibility. But it is wise at least to question someone's honesty if that person acts confused about a clear ethical issue.

righteous feed many, But fools die for lack of wisdom." The honest person is constantly saying positive words (*choice silver*) that energize people. He does not say whatever he feels without restraint. Unlike the wicked who vomit up words like molten lava on others without thinking or intentionally harm or intimidate ("where words are many sin is not lacking"), the wise person carefully says true things at the right moment to inspire and challenge others. Sometimes the words are not always easy to hear, particularly, for example, when presenting bad news about job performance. But even these tough words can have a positive impact in the long run when received by a wise person, who will learn from the situation.

Proverbs 11:1 - "Dishonest scales are an abomination to the Lord, But a just weight is His delight." This is one of several verses contained in Proverbs that speaks of honesty in the actual practice of business (which is the arena where much dishonesty can take place as "standard" business practices). You give customers what you say you will give them with no hidden agenda. There is no room for falsely inflating prices based on whatever you can get away with. Obviously, in a free market, you can set your prices to whatever the market will bear. This verse talks about false practices such as *bait and switch* (advertising a certain price for a certain item but not providing it and offering a more expensive item).[54] Setting honest prices, providing what you say you will provide, doing what you say you will do for the customer, and paying bills on time as promised are all keys to carrying out honesty in business.

Proverbs 17:19 - "He who loves transgression loves strife, And he who exalts his gate seeks destruction." Dishonesty has an impact. The dishonest person (*he who loves transgression*) will stir up conflict among others. They *love strife*. Some leaders think conflict is good.[55] However,

---

[54] Some would disagree with me, but I would add deceptive packaging to this category; having a large box, for example, that when opened is half full. I realize that contents *settle*, but it is a technique that can confuse customers, not to mention the lack of stewardship for the environment of adding unnecessary waste.

[55] This leadership approach is based on the Darwinian idea of *survival of the fittest*. You purposefully introduce conflict (like a *predator*) in order to put pressure on

the honest person will try to communicate openly and honestly as often as possible to those who need to hear.

Main Principle #3: Be Wise

Christianity is very realistic.[56] So in business, the Christian realizes that she will deal with unethical people. The scriptures teach us to be *wise as serpents*[57] as we work with these kinds of people. This means that organizations need to implement a system of checks and balances to hold people accountable to organizational standards. This is particularly important in a business area such as accounting. The Christian leader must stay true to high principles of business ethics (as we are discussing) and uphold them, while still making a profit. This takes wisdom! Let's look at Proverbs.[58]

---

others to act in a certain way. Your goal is to keep people off balance so that you can maintain control through intimidation. There is a place for putting pressure on people to bring out their best. The pressure should come, however, not by deceit but by showing others the reality of their situation (based on company ethical standards and company mission) in a way that challenges them. The writer of the Proverbs refers to the Darwinian type of businessperson who uses strife to solidify his own political position within the organization.

[56] See 1 John 2:1, "These things I write to you, so that you may not sin. *And if anyone sins*, we have an Advocate with the Father, Jesus Christ the righteous." (emphasis added) John tells us in chapter 1 that we must not sin against God. He does not want us to fall prey to the temptations of the Evil One. But John is also concerned that if we do sin that we do not fall prey to the second *punch* of the Evil One; accusation. He reminds us (realizing that people will sin) that Christ will forgive us and help us as He promised.

[57] See Matthew 10:16 where Jesus sends his disciples out of the fellowship of other Christians and into the world "of wolves" (like the business world). As He does this, He tells them: "'Behold, I send you out as sheep in the midst of wolves. Therefore be wise as serpents and harmless as doves." The notion (also very true for business) is that as a Christian you must be very smart in dealing with unethical people while not losing your own ethical standards.

[58] Other verses that talk about wisdom in business (or give examples of wise behavior) include: Proverbs 1:14, 15; 1:25; 2:7; 2:12; 3:7, 8:18; 12:1; 12:22; 13:5; 17:1; 17:10; 17:19; 17:23; 19:5; 19:9; 20:10; 27:12; 28:4; 28:13.

Proverbs 3:16-18 characterizes wisdom as, "Length of days is in her right hand, In her left hand riches and honor. Her ways are ways of pleasantness, And all her paths are peace. She is a tree of life to those who take hold of her, And happy are all who retain her." This passage simply emphasizes the benefits of wisdom. Wise leadership produces a positive environment in the work place.[59]

Proverbs 4:19 - "The way of the wicked is like darkness; They do not know what makes them stumble." This passage addresses the repercussions resulting from a lack of wisdom. There is an obstruction to understanding. This result has two ramifications for the wise person. If you work with an unethical leader, it can help you understand the chaos and confusion that permeates the atmosphere. If you are a leader, it can help explain the confusion in doing business with certain people.

Proverbs 19:20 - "Listen to counsel and receive instruction, That you may be wise in your latter days." A wise leader proactively turns to wise people for advice. This is smart because it is impossible to know everything. One of the marks of a great leader is that when he faces a difficult situation he seeks advice from the right person who has strengths to help in just that situation.

Proverbs 26:23-26

> Fervent lips with a wicked heart are like earthenware covered with silver dross. He who hates, disguises it with his lips, And lays up deceit within himself. When he speaks kindly, do not believe him, For there are seven abominations in his heart;

---

[59] Notice the reference to the *tree of life*. This is a very powerful statement about the importance of wisdom. The author is saying that unlike Eve (and Adam certainly concurred) who foolishly (against God's clear command) listened to the Evil One when he lied and said that eating of the fruit of the forbidden tree of life would bring insight and life; listening to and obeying God (which is *real wisdom*) will ultimately allow one to know God's thoughts (the original desire of Eve and Adam) and have life. Things have not changed. We need God's perspective to have a True understanding of life even today.

> Though his hatred is covered by deceit, His wickedness will
> be revealed before the assembly.

This passage highlights a situation that demands wisdom by the leader. We need wisdom to discern accurately and do the right thing. This is a situation where someone is nice and speaks kindly and is passionate (fervent) about what he believes. However at bottom line, the goal of this person is to deceive because their heart is full of hate. The wise person recognizes this and sets up a group situation (where all can discern and critique) to expose the deceit.

The entire book of Proverbs speaks of wisdom. The main emphasis of this principle (#3) however, is to discern duplicity in business so that your business does not suffer. As one business man (in banking) summed it up so well (in balancing the kind, loving attitude we want as Christians with business smarts), "trust everyone and check everything." The honest person will not mind being checked out because they are telling the truth. The dishonest person will be found out, which protects the business. This is wisdom in action.

Main Principle #4: Be Diligent

Christianity condemns laziness, especially if done in the name of religion.[60] Paul recommended a welfare policy for society (as a basic starting point) when he wrote (2 Thessalonians 3:10), "If anyone will

---

[60] See 1 Thessalonians 4:11, "that you also aspire to lead a quiet life, to mind your own business, and to work with your own hands, as we commanded you." Evidently there were people in the church of Thessalonica who did not work but spent their time gossiping about *spiritual* things. This practice upset the church and caused the perpetrators to expect handouts from others for their livelihood.

See also 1 Timothy 5:13, "And besides they [young widows] learn to be idle, wandering about from house to house, and not only idle but also gossips and busybodies, saying things which they ought not." (brackets added) Again, probably under the guise of doing *spiritual things*, they disrupt the church instead of carrying out productive work.

not work, neither shall he eat." Here are verses found in Proverbs on diligence.[61]

Proverbs 10:4 - "He who has a slack hand becomes poor, But the hand of the diligent makes rich." There is a direct relationship between hard work and riches. The lazy person wants to take short cuts to wealth. The "short cut" often leads to unethical behavior. The idea behind diligence is that you persevere in doing the right thing, confident that in the long run you will produce tangible results.

Proverbs 10:26 - "As vinegar to the teeth and smoke to the eyes, So is the lazy man to those who send him." This verse paints a vivid picture using a simile showing that you are very foolish to trust a lazy man. You are simply hurting and fooling yourself in the long run if you think you can depend on a lazy person.

Proverbs 24:30-34

> I went by the field of the lazy man, And by the vineyards of the man devoid of understanding; And there it was, all overgrown with thorns; Its surface was covered with nettles; Its stone wall was broken down. When I saw it, I considered it well; I looked on it and received instruction: A little sleep, a little slumber, A little folding of the hands to rest; So shall your poverty come like a prowler, And your need like an armed man.

This salient illustration shows the link between laziness and poverty. The lazy person does nothing to improve their God-given property. They do not take seriously God's calling to have dominion[62] (which means to responsibly use the things God gives you). They prefer sleep and leisure, and the result is poverty.

---

[61] Other verses include: Proverbs 1:32; 6:6-11; 10:16; 12:11; 12:24; 13:4; 14:23; 15:19; 19:15; 19:24; 20:4; 21:5,6

[62] See Genesis 1:26, "Then God said, 'Let Us make man in Our image, according to Our likeness, let them have dominion over the fish of the sea, over the birds of the air, and over the cattle, over all the earth."

Main Principle #5: Do Good To People

We are to intentionally do good to all of the people with whom we do business including employees, customers, vendors, stockholders, and the community around us. This is particularly true about those, from these groups, who are poor. The Biblical concept of justice summarizes this concept of doing good to others.[63] Chewning (1990) describes justice as, "a deep concern for the well being of the poor ... especially the defenseless. They [companies] must together work to build structures that protect the rights of everyone and take care of the weakest people" (p. 28) (brackets added).

The Scriptures condemn the mistreatment of others, particularly in the work place.[64] We are to show understanding and provide help to people who have real needs (not ones that are in need because of a refusal to work).[65] Unfortunately, work can become a means of oppressing and defrauding workers.[66] This is unacceptable. The Scriptures remind us that "The laborer is worthy of his hire." (Luke 10:7) The Biblical picture is one where there is mutual respect and hard work from employers and

---

[63] See chapter 7 for a more in-depth discussion of how organizations can help those around them.

[64] See Exodus 22:21, "You shall neither mistreat a stranger nor oppress him, for you were strangers in the land of Egypt." See especially Isaiah 58 where God condemns Israel for following the religious ritual of fasting while behaving abominably, particularly in the work place: (verse 3) "... In fact in the day of your fast you find pleasure, And exploit all your laborers." This is totally unacceptable.

[65] Also, keep in mind that (per our previous discussion in this book) a *need* is defined as food and clothing (shelter). See passages on diligence.

[66] See Exodus 1:11-14 and 2:23 where the Egyptians treated the Israelites severely despite their productivity. See also James 5:4 where God accuses the rich of fraud. Apparently the *Christians* referred to in James 5:4 not only forced laborers to work on the Sabbath (note reference to "Lord of the Sabbath" insinuating that God was also personally insulted by this wrong action of making people work on the Sabbath) but to add insult to injury, withheld their wages: "Indeed the wages of the laborers who mowed your fields, which you kept back by fraud, cry out; and the cries of the reapers have reached the ears of the Lord of the Sabbath."

employees driven by a common loyalty to Christ and His principles.[67] Paul reminds us that this concern for others applies in non-profit situations as well.[68]

The Bible also gives a pattern for businesses regarding concern for others and how to demonstrate that concern. The book of Ruth gives one example as part of its narrative, to leave some of the goods produced for the poor.[69] Deuteronomy is even more specific about exactly how to treat poor workers (particularly immigrants or aliens).[70] Employers must actively consider the situations of their workers.

The New Testament suggests that concern for others (especially ones who appear more lowly) is a fundamental tenet of Christianity,

---

[67] See Ephesians 6:5-9, "Bondservants, be obedient to those who are your masters according to the flesh, with fear and trembling, in sincerity of heart, as to Christ; not with eye service, as men-pleasers, but as bondservants of Christ, doing the will of God from the heart, with goodwill doing service, as to the Lord, and not to men, knowing that whatever good anyone does, he will receive the same from the Lord, whether he is a slave or free. And you, masters, do the same things to them, giving up threatening, knowing that your own Master also is in heaven, and there is no partiality with Him."

[68] See 1 Thessalonians 2:9-12 where Paul worked night and day so that he could better serve his organization: "For you remember, brethren, our labor and toil; for laboring night and day, that we might not be a burden to any of you, we preached to you the gospel of God. You are witnesses, and God also, how devoutly and justly and blamelessly we behaved ourselves among you who believe; as you know how we exhorted, and comforted, and charged every one of you, as a father does his own children, that you would walk worthy of God who calls you into His own kingdom and glory." This is a non-profit situation but notice Paul's persistence in finding some way to develop His people; truly demonstrating a transformational leadership approach.

[69] See Ruth 2:6-8 where Boaz had a policy of allowing poor people to *glean* from his field (taking the extra grain missed by the main harvest). See further explanation and application of this principle in chapter 7 of this book.

[70] See Deuteronomy 24:14-15, "You shall not oppress a hired servant who is poor and needy, whether one of your brethren or one of the aliens who is in you land within your gates. Each day you shall give him his wages, and not let the sun go down on it, for he is poor and has set his heart on it; lest he cry out against you to the Lord, and it be sin to you." See also Deuteronomy 24:21 where gleaning is directed (not just suggested as the Ruth narrative indicates), "When you gather the grapes of your vineyard, you shall not glean it afterward; it shall be for the stranger, the fatherless, and the widow."

because we are all made in God's image and thus are valuable.[71] Now let's look at more passages from the perspective of Proverbs.[72]

Proverbs 3:27 - "Do not withhold good from those to whom it is due, When it is in the power of your hand to do so." This verse highlights the essential need for concern for those with whom you work. The idea of Christianity is that you do good for the moment, and also purposefully (strategically) seek out ways to do good for those around you in the future.

Proverbs 11:25, 27 - "The generous soul will be made rich, And he who waters will also be watered himself. ... He who earnestly seeks good finds favor, But trouble will come to him who seeks evil." This verse is one of the Biblical sources of the slogan; "what goes around, comes around." As you do good to others, you build genuine good will. And just as assuredly, the one who does evil will eventually find trouble.

Proverbs 17:13, 15 - "Whoever rewards evil for good, Evil will not depart from his house. ... He who justifies the wicked, and he who condemns the just, Both of them alike are an abomination to the Lord." This verse is particularly telling because it covers the situation when leaders (those who reward) confuse their values by rewarding evil and punishing good. The point of the passage is that you are building a foundation for disaster when you manage this way. You will face evil yourself. This was demonstrated at Enron where the CFO made big bonuses for setting up unethical (though technically legal) entities for hiding debt. Rewarding this kind of duplicity backfired in the long run with the demise of Enron and the prosecution of the CFO.

---

[71] See Matthew 25:40, "... 'Inasmuch as you did it to one of the least of these My brethren, you did it to me.'" See also Matthew 25:35-46 where serving others who are less fortunate is like serving Christ himself, especially verses 35-36, "... 'for I was hungry and you gave Me food; I was thirsty and you gave Me drink; I was a stranger and you took Me in; I was naked and you clothed Me; I was sick and you visited Me; I was in prison and you came to Me.'"

[72] Other verses include: Proverbs 3:3; 6:30-31; 11:10, 12; 11:17; 14:21; 14:31; 15:22; 16:26; 18:2; 18:5; 18:17, 19; 19:17; 20:5; 21:15; 21:13; 21:26; 22:16; 24:24; 25:21; 28:15-16; 28:21; 29:19; 29:24; 28:27.

In some ways, it takes much more energy to manage an unethical company. You are always looking over your shoulder, knowing that others are plotting evil against you (which can be true according to this Scripture). This situation produces a confusing organizational environment because you are treating the wrong people well; the ones who are acting unethically. This is foolishness because it is an affront to the God of justice and because a business cannot keep making money within the confines of this sort of organizational culture. Proverbs recommends that you reward those who do good and put pressure on those who do the wrong thing to change their wrong behavior, leave the organization, or be punished.

Proverbs 18:1 - "A man who isolates himself seeks his own desire; He rages against all wise judgment." This verse underscores the need for showing concern for people by valuing their opinions. It is wise to do so. The foolish CEO trusts only his gut[73]and ignores wise advice from ethical people in his organization. This is normally a formula for disaster. You do not want a person like this as head of your organization because, even though charismatic, he can ultimately be selfish and only looking out for his own interests. This person will do fine as long as things are going well. But under pressure, which is when you want a great leader to perform greatly, this person will ignore the interests of others. If the ship is sinking, he will make sure that he is the first one to leave, with all his money in tact, leaving others to suffer the consequences of his failure.

Proverbs 22:22-23 - "Do not rob the poor because he is poor, Nor oppress the afflicted at the gate; For the Lord will plead their cause, And plunder the soul of those who plunder them." and Proverbs 29:7 - "The righteous considers the cause of the poor, But the wicked does not understand such knowledge." These verses speaks loudly and clearly that we should not exploit the poor in business nor deliberately keep (oppress) them from progressing financially. This does not mean that

---

[73] It is possible that if a leader has a solid Christian worldview, then their gut reaction will reflect it which is OK. Also, certain leaders have a certain feeling in their gut about business decisions which is OK, but may not include ethics which is not OK.

you need to artificially give them more than is due.[74] However, it is important that you treat the poor fairly and not take advantage of or profit from their difficult situations.

Proverbs 28:3 - "A poor man who oppresses the poor is like a driving rain which leaves no food." This verse underscores the reality that others oppress besides the rich. Peers who are elevated to management positions can sometimes act with more pride and oppression over their own group than outsiders. It is particularly disheartening ("like a driving rain") to workers when one of their own is put in a management position and then they exploit others as much or more than the rich leaders. This can be a problem particularly in union situations where union leaders (who are supposed to help workers) use the money of workers (from union dues) to make themselves rich and to pursue their own political positions.

We can conclude our analysis of Proverbs by looking at Proverbs 30:8-9 (notice how similar it is to the passage in Philippians 4): "Remove falsehood and lies far from me; Give me neither poverty nor riches - Feed me with the food allotted to me; Lest I be full and deny You, And say, 'Who is the Lord?' Or lest I be poor and steal, And profane the name of my God." Contentment through trust in the principles that God gives us; this is the underlying principle of business ethics according to the Scriptures.

THE PROTESTANT WORK ETHIC

In concluding this section, I want to comment briefly on the Protestant work ethic as a reflection of the Biblical view towards work and thus business ethics. The Protestant work ethic closely, but not completely, represents this Biblical perspective. Cavanagh (1998) summarizes the

---

[74] See the parable of the laborers (Matthew 20:1 ff.) where the landowner paid workers a denarius, a normal (fair) days wage (no more or less), for that time period. See Burkett's chapter on fair wages in his book on business, *Business by the Book.*

Protestant work ethic[75] as focusing on hard work (diligence), seeing work as a calling from God, and the fact that reinvestment was OK. (p. 115) He also lists: "self-control, self-reliance, perseverance, saving and planning ahead, and honesty ('observing the rules of the game')" (Cavanagh, 1998, p. 117). In summary, the Protestant work ethic sees the importance of hard work in the long run and that faith and work do integrate: "In his last chapter Weber quotes founding Protestants John Wesley and John Calvin when they point out a paradox. It is religion that makes people careful, hardworking, frugal; and this, in turn enables them to build up wealth" (Cavanagh, 1998, p. 117).[76]

Thus the Protestant Work ethic and the Christian foundation provide a rationally[77] complete system for business ethics. Historically, this ethical foundation has been a key factor to fuel economic prosperity.[78]

---

[75] He (Cavanagh, 1998, p. 115) cites the work of John Calvin as providing the most important influence on these ideas, later adopted by American settlers. However, Cavanagh's understanding of the teachings of John Calvin is somewhat askew. For example, Luther also believed in predestination because it is taught in the Scriptures (Romans 8; Ephesians 1). Also, Calvin does not believe that predestination means *a small number* will believe. This is a matter of perspective. God promised Abraham a people (these are Believers, see Galatians 3:6-9, 26-29) "as many as the stars in the sky." But, as Cavanagh suggests, this does not include all mankind so could be considered *small*.

[76] Cavanagh is citing the work of Max Weber on the Protestant work ethic. See also Proverbs 22:29 that highlights the worthiness of work, "Do you see a man who excels in his work? He will stand before kings; He will not stand before unknown men."

[77] Sire (1990) comments on this rationality, "If we follow out the hints readily available in the world around us, we find that the belief that this God really exists is not based on wishful thinking but is quite rational, quite reasonable. It may not be strictly provable like a mathematical formula, but it can be justified like a verdict in a court of law. When the rules of evidence are all properly in operation, a reasonable verdict can be rendered" (p. 107).

[78] That is why it is so tragic to see how work has been demeaned in modern politics/culture.

CHAPTER 3 QUESTIONS FOR REVIEW

1. Why don't Christians believe that their faith can apply in the work environment?
2. Why is the Covenant the foundation for Biblical business ethics?
3. Describe the Covenant.
4. Describe key components of the Biblical view of work. What are the ramifications for business ethics?; for personnel function?; for the economy? Give one or two examples.
5. Why is an understanding of the principles of Ecclesiastes so important to a Biblical perspective on business and business ethics?
6. What does Ecclesiastes say about purpose and satisfaction? Give two or three verses as examples.
7. What does 1 Timothy 6 say about the role of wealth?
8. What does Philippians 4:10-13 say about contentment?
9. Review the 5 Main Principles, principles that are important in understanding a Biblical view of business ethics along with Scriptural examples. Give examples of how you have (or might in the future) apply these principles.
10. Give a brief explanation of the Protestant Work Ethics and its importance to economic growth.

UNDERSTAND THE ETHICS OF OTHERS

MANY WOULD SAY THAT THERE is **no** relationship between faith and business ethics. Guy (1990) argues that it (ethics) "… is different from religion because it makes no theological assumptions." (p. 4) One of my students in his class evaluation of my business ethics class wrote (basically), "You have to quit talking about religion and philosophy so much and talk about ethics." I would argue (as discussed previously) just the opposite; that ethics has everything to do with religion and philosophy. I would agree that "The issue [in life in general and business ethics in particular] is not whether we live by faith, *but in whom or in what we place our faith*"[1] (Chewning, Eby, & Shirley, 1990, p 7) (emphasis added) (brackets added). Everyone has a "religion"; something or someone they trust in to make life work.[2] We will continue to examine the nature of that something or someone in this chapter as it applies to our personal business ethics, the ethics of others and also as it applies to the ethics of the organization.

We have examined the particulars of a Christian view of business ethics as an example of how one can draw from their worldview and

---

[1] This is why (as we shall see later) that the Christian approach to business ethics is, I think, a very honest approach. It fully recognizes that **all** of us live by faith, but the important question is; what is the **object** of your faith? Christianity sees it as the real life, death, and resurrection of Jesus Christ in history. Secularists put their trust in luck, astrology, in themselves alone, other people, or government (just to name a few).

[2] Secularists (who are discussed in this chapter) argue that they are not religious; but they simply place themselves as the, in this case, object of faith and "who" they trust in to make life work.

relate it to business ethics. Now we will examine other ethical systems. The list is not exhaustive but highlights ethical ("normative ethics") viewpoints often associated with business ethics, along with a look at culture and "where we are" ethically. Keep in mind that you may not agree with the views presented in this chapter. It is OK. But they are important to understand because many people hold these views (maybe unknowingly) and you need to do business with all kinds of people. The more you understand the ethical views of others (see Ruddell model from chapter 1), the wiser you will be in interactions with them, which should give you a competitive advantage. It will also help with risk management and knowing when there is NOT a "common ground for doing business" with another individual or organization. Thus, you will avoid the time and effort and cost associated with trying to manage a bad fit.

SECULAR VIEW OF ETHICS

We will begin by looking at more traditional secular views of ethical standards. Then we will examine other views that seem to hold a bigger influence in today's business culture.

Utilitarianism

Utilitarianism is a secular theory that emerged in the 1800s as a practical way to make ethical decisions without having to appeal to religion. Bentham and Mill (who we draw from in this chapter) are credited with developing the approach. It was a "practical" approach in that it avoided having to determine any eternal standards of right and wrong but looked instead at the consequences of actions. Utilitarianism sees an action as good if it produces good consequences. Good is determined by how much an action maximizes pleasure and minimizes pain.[3] Mill

---

[3] "To give a clear view of the moral standard set up by the theory, much more requires to be said; in particular, what things it includes in the ideas of pain

highlighted two types of utilitarianism: *act* and *rule*. Act utilitarianism looks at the consequences of each act to determine good (individual ethics) while rule utilitarianism looks at the result of rules (ethics of the organization or societal laws).

For Mill, good is seen as whatever produces the greatest good for the greatest number of people. In a sense, this approach encourages fairness because it does not want to sacrifice the well-being of the many for the convenience of, for example, the elite or powerful. However, historically, there has been a problem determining exactly what is *good*. Bentham introduced the idea that the good could be quantified. So, theoretically, people can identify any action or belief as good as long as it measured up even though Mill tried to avoid this arbitrary view by distinguishing different levels of pleasure. At bottom line, motivation is not important. What is important is to try to accomplish the greatest good for the greatest number given the circumstances.

As we seek to apply utilitarianism to modern issues, the good can take different forms. In business, the good is often determined by what makes the greatest amount of money. Many think that this led the Ford Motor company in the late 1960s to leave off a $10 part on a Pinto that was needed to keep the gasoline tank from exploding on impact when hit from behind. The calculation was that it would be cheaper for Ford to pay fines and penalties and settlements from resulting accidents than to recall all Pintos and add the part. The good became a calculation.

How could this work in the business of sports? In Major League Baseball, for example, the use of steroids appeared to be ignored for a number of years, leading to a spike in home run output and the shattering of Roger Maris' 35+ year season home run record. It also lead

---

and pleasure; and to what extent this is left an open question. ... But these supplementary explanations do not affect the theory of life on which this theory of morality is grounded - namely, that pleasure, and freedom from pain, are the only things desirable as ends; and that all desirable things (which are as numerous in the utilitarian as in any other scheme) are desirable either for the pleasure inherent in themselves, or as means to the promotion of pleasure and the prevention of pain." (Mill, 1879, p. 11)

to Most Valuable Player (MVP) awards for the likes of Ken Caminiti (San Diego Padres at the time). When the investigation finally took place beginning in 2007, there was a voice of cooperation "for the good of the game." In others words, you could say that removing steroids from the league became good when the potential pain of losing attendance and suffering legal repercussions became so great that it would harm those involved in the game. Obviously, there were many other issues at stake in this case, but certainly a utilitarian perspective was one of them.

Utilitarianism can also be used to manipulate. Mill notes that "the good" should not focus on one's own desire for happiness but "the greatest happiness altogether."[4] This can result in a problem that is opposite to the one stated above, where individuality is considered "wrong" and performers work harder and harder to contribute for those who aren't performing. Mill would not argue for this outcome, yet seems to recognize its possibility.[5]

Mill advances a utopian notion[6] that people, if trained properly, will want to do what is best for others.[7] This is certainly an admirable idea.

---

[4] "But it is by no means an indispensable condition to the acceptance of the utilitarian standard; *for that standard is not the agent's own greatest happiness, but the greatest happiness altogether*; and if it may possibly be doubted whether a noble character is always the happier for its nobleness, there can be no doubt that it makes other people happier, and that the world in general is immensely a gainer by it." (Mill, 1879, p. 17) (emphasis added)

[5] "The utilitarian morality does recognize in human beings the power of sacrificing their own greatest good for the good of others. It only refuses to admit that the sacrifice is itself a good. A sacrifice which does not increase, or tend to increase, the sum total of happiness, it considers as wasted." (Mill, 1879, p. 25) He assumes that those who are receiving the benefit are not taking advantage of it. We would hope that this is the case ... but a basic law of economics is that people respond to incentives. So, if they have no reason for trying harder to receive benefit, why should they?

[6] "The corollaries from the principle of utility, like the precepts of every practical art, admit of indefinite improvement, and, in a progressive state of the human mind, their improvement is perpetually going on." (Mill, 1879, p. 36)

[7] "As the means of making the nearest approach to this ideal, utility would enjoin, first, that laws and social arrangements should place the happiness ... of every individual ... in harmony with the interest of the whole; and secondly, that

But education doesn't necessarily make people more ethical unless tied to ethical leadership.[8] So this is a potential limitation as well.

Another issue with Utilitarianism is the problem of unintended consequences. This problem is tied to other secular ideologies as well. We may think that we know what will best benefit the most people, but a decision can create other problems that end up making things worse. Enron serves as an example here. Andy Fastow (former Enron CFO) most likely convinced himself that he was "helping" the "greater good" by setting up phony entities to funnel money into Enron (and himself!). But this decision (actually series of decisions) resulted in unintended consequences; Enron's failure.

Deontology

Immanuel Kant was a Prussian (what is now part of Germany) philosopher who wrote in the 1700s. Inspired by the Scottish philosopher David Hume, Kant turned his analytical mind to epistemology (how we know what we know) and ultimately to ethics. When his book *Critique of Pure Reason* was released around 1775, some say that it had more impact on the world than the Declaration of Independence and the Revolutionary War that followed that birthed the United States of America (Sproul, 1993). Kant himself understood the impact of his ideas and compared his ideas and the resulting change in philosophy (by shifting the basis for metaphysics and resulting epistemology from God to man) with Copernicus and the change in science when he confirmed that the Earth revolves around the Sun and not vice versa. Kant contributed to modern ethics by advocating common standards

---

education and opinion, which have so vast a power over human character, should so use that power as to establish in the mind of every individual an indissoluble association between his own happiness and the good of the whole ..." (Mill, 1879, p. 26)

[8] See 1 Peter 5:1-3 and note the focus on modeling ethical character as a way to develop people versus simply passing on information (education): "... shepherd the flock of God that is among you, exercising oversight ... being examples to the flock." (ESV)

that rational people can and should abide by.[9] He argues that ethics does not come simply from "human volition" (one's own will), but of something greater.[10]

However, Kant rejected historical arguments for the belief in God and the acceptance of revealed Truth from God as the way to truly understand the world around us. Kant began his argument by starting with man and man's reason.[11] Based on reason, man can understand the world around him, what Kant calls the *phenomenal* realm or what we can experience day to day (how things appear to us). But Kant said that rationally we cannot know anything definite beyond what we can see and experience; or what he called the *noumenal* realm. He didn't necessarily reject God or universal considerations for reality but he in essence dismissed them[12] because he came to the conclusion that we just cannot fathom this noumenal world because of the limits of our reason.[13] What we can know truly is what we can see and experience and evaluate based on our reason. This idea had significant ramifications for ethics.[14]

---

[9] "Everyone must admit that if a law is to have moral force, i.e., to be the basis of an obligation, it must carry with it absolute necessity ... therefore, the basis of obligation must not be sought in the nature of man, or in the circumstances in the world in which he is placed, but a priori simply in the conception of pure reason; and although any other precept which if founded on principles of mere experience may be in certain respects universal. When applied to man, it does not borrow the least thing from the knowledge of many himself (anthropology), but gives laws a priori to him as a rational being." (Kant, 1785, p. ii)

[10] "For the metaphysic of morals has to examine the idea and the principles of a possible pure will, and not the acts and conditions of human volition generally, which for the most part are drawn from psychology." (Kant, 1785, p. iv)

[11] "Logic cannot have any empirical part; that is, a part in which the universal and necessary laws of thought should rest on grounds taken from experience; otherwise it would not be logic ..." (Kant, 1785, p. 1).

[12] "A will whose maxims necessarily coincide with the laws of autonomy is a holy will, good absolutely." (Kant, 1785, p. 103)

[13] "In a practical philosophy ... it is not the reasons of what happens that we have to ascertain ..." (Kant, 1785, p. 75).

[14] However, ironically, Kant insisted on "a good will" (giving a nod to Biblical Truth of the need for a new heart, see 2nd Corinthians 5:17): "Nothing can

Kant argued that we can't really look to any universal standard because, as stated previously, we can't know anything about it based on "rational" pursuit. However when it comes to ethics, we have to act as if there is a God because, as Kant argues, without a God representing an eternal standard of right and wrong, there is no basis for ethics. So in his work on ethics, Kant built a system based on rationality, called *deontology* (or duty).[15] In other words, we do what is right because of duty, because, and only because, it is the right thing to do.[16] We are not concerned about motives or consequences.[17] We make a choice solely based on principle. Kant's main rule for determining the *right* was the *categorical imperative*. It basically states that we should act in such a way that if everyone else acted that way (in other words became a universal norm) then it would be acceptable. So standards come from what is collectively agreed upon rather than what is beneficial for a particular group at a particular time or what is good for the greatest number of people. A corollary was to treat people as ends and not means. In other

---

possibly be conceived in the world, or even out of it, which can be called good, without qualification, except a good will." (Kant, 1785, p. 1) He then goes on to list positive character qualities and say: "… but these gifts of nature may also become extremely bad and mischievous if the will which is to make use of them, and which, therefore, constitutes character, is not good." (Kant, 1785, p. 1)

[15] For example; "To be beneficent when we can *is a duty*; …" (Kant, 1785, p. 11). (emphasis added)

[16] "For in order that an action should be morally good, it is not enough that it conform to the moral law, but it must also be done for the sake of the law …" (Kant, 1785, p. 9). "We have then to develop the notion of a will which deserves to be highly esteemed for itself and is good without a view to anything further, a notion which exists already in the sound natural understanding …" (Kant, 1785, p. 9). Kant seems to draw on "borrowed capital" here which is "borrowing" from God's goodness and creation and righteous standards as a basis for, in this case, "good" yet without acknowledging Him as the source.

[17] "The second proposition is: That an action done from duty derives its moral worth, not from the purpose which is to be attained by it [i.e. end results], but from the maxim by which it is determined …" (Kant, 1785, p. 15). (brackets added) "Thus the worth of an action does not lie in the effect expected from it, nor in any principle of action which requires to borrow its motive from this expected effect." (Kant, 1785, p. 17)

words, we should respect people and not use them. Kant's view leads to the notion that people have rights (to be treated as ends and not means) and duties (to do the right thing).

The business of sports can illustrate Kant's ideas. The presence of rules in sports and the importance of adhering to those rules reflects duty and devotion to duty. Perhaps the best example of Kantian ethics in sports is golf. Players are to follow the rules explicitly and volunteer information when they have violated the rules, even unwittingly. For example, touching a sand trap with a club before striking the ball is a penalty and needs to be reported. Greg Chalmers, from Australia, demonstrated this devotion to duty in the 2002 Professional Golfer Association (PGA) Kemper Insurance Open tournament. On Sunday night, after the 3rd round of the tournament (played on Sunday due to rain), Chalmers realized he had make a costly mistake. During the round earlier in the day, an opposing player's caddy kept looking at Chalmers' bag to determine the club he was using, an action that was impolite but technically not illegal. After a poor shot, Chalmers replaced his club and the opposing player's caddy looked again, Chalmers in frustration audibly mentioned the club he used. After the round, Chalmers happened to hear about a similar incident. He also realized that audibly mentioning a club is illegal because it is against the rules to give advice to an opponent resulting in a 2 stroke penalty. The next day, he reported the error and unfortunately he had to default from the tournament because he noticed the error late and thus had signed his scorecard with the wrong score, again a rule violation. He ended up losing close to $100,000 of what he would have earned if he had been able to compete on the 4th and final round on Monday and maintain his position. Ironically, if the tournament had ended on Sunday as planned, Chalmers could have kept his winnings because the reported violation would have occurred too late to resolve. Why would someone do this? Deontology demands that we do something because it is the right thing to do.

In making decisions with the Kantian approach, you constantly ask: what is right? Following the rules is important and trying to do what is right is important no matter what others are doing. We are to constantly ask ourselves, what if what I am doing is adapted by everyone, how would that impact my sport or business? We are concerned about the integrity of the game or the foundation of the economy, that it is played as the rules require.

One potential pitfall of deontology is that it can lead to legalism (see chapter 5). In other words, there is such a focus on the rules, that there is no consideration of the purpose of the rules or motives. This can happen with organizational codes of conduct that contain long lists of what not to do, but no guidance as to what TO do. It can also lead to bureaucracy where people elevate procedures to "ethical standards." Also, rules don't make people better.[18] That is a matter of the heart and requires a good character; something Kant alludes to but gives no guidance as to how to gain an ethical heart beyond ourselves. Finally, rules can be used to manipulate people to do evil. For example, German leaders were "following rules" (laws passed by the government) in discriminating against and killing Jews during World War II. Of course, the fatal flaw of deontology is that it removes God from ethics but tries to "borrow" form natural law (God's law) when advocating universal standards of "duty." Western philosophy quickly realized that if God is removed, there is no basis for a universal standard of right and wrong (Sproul, 1993).

Virtue Theory

Ancient Greece serves as the background for *Virtue* ethics. We could argue that this view has historically had a large influence on western culture. What are its tenants? How does it compare and contrast with other secular views?

Virtue ethics focuses on thinking as the guide for right and wrong and balance ("golden mean") between excesses. Aristotle does seek to

---

[18] See Colossians 2:20-23, "... do you submit to regulations – 'Do not handle, Do not taste, Do not touch' [referring to things that all perish as they are used] - according to human precepts and teachings? These have indeed an **appearance** of wisdom ... but they are **of no value in stopping the indulgence of the flesh**." (ESV) (bold and brackets added)

ask the right questions: "The 'morals and vices' make up what we call character, and the important questions arise: (1) What is character? and (2) How is it formed [through habit]? (For character in this sense is not a natural endowment; it is formed or produced)."[19] (circa 340 B.C.) (brackets added) Also, he acknowledges the importance of mentors in developing character: "The process [for how to form character] is one of assimilation, largely by imitation and under direction and control."[20] (Aristotle, circa 340 B.C.) (brackets added)

For Aristotle the answer to the question; "what is the standard"?; is happiness from the gods. "Now to be sure, if anything else is a gift of the Gods to men, it is probably that Happiness is a gift of theirs too, and especially because of all human goods it is the highest." (Aristotle, circa 340 B.C.)[21] And happiness can be explained as, pleasures and pains.[22] Here virtue theory seems to coincide with Utilitarianism in focusing on pleasure and pain as the basis for human behavior (and ethics). But, Aristotle also seems to tie happiness to conduct, "For to constitute Happiness, there must be, as we have said, complete virtue and a complete life; ..." (Aristotle, circa 340 B.C.).[23] In contrast, the

---

[19] This would be in line with the Biblical view to the extent that good character is not normal but must be developed (see Ephesians 4:17 ff. and the importance of "putting off" old ways and "putting on" new ways). However, Aristotle does not acknowledge original sin, so there is no acknowledgement that people have no interest/power in doing the right thing for the right reason without Christ.

[20] This is consistent with the Biblical notion of discipleship (see 2 Timothy 2:2) but, again, the basis for the modeling is suspect without eternal standards of right and wrong. So, we are left with appealing to "reason" as the standard: "But what are 'right' acts? In the first place, they are those that conform to a rule – the right rule, and ultimately to reason." (Aristotle, circa 340 BC)

[21] See also his statement, "... in fact every excellence we choose for their own sakes .... conceiving that through their instrumentality we shall be happy. ... So then Happiness is manifestly something final and self-sufficient, being the end of all things which are and may be done." (Aristotle, circa 340 B.C.)

[22] "For Moral Virtue has for its object-matter pleasures and pains, because by reason of pleasure we do what is bad, and by reason of pain decline doing what is right." (Aristotle, circa 340 B.C.)

[23] We could say that this idea that virtue leads to happiness is a vague reflection of the more precise statement in Matthew 6:33 where God commands us to seek His

Scriptures highlight a right understanding of God and our relationship with Him and desire to please Him as the basis for ethics; "I therefore, a prisoner for the Lord, urge you to walk in a manner worthy of the calling to which you have been called, ..." (Ephesians 4:1, ESV).

So, where does this standard of happiness come from for Aristotle? Apparently, it comes from within as we derive it from culture. "The Virtues then come to be in us neither by nature, nor in spite of nature, but we are furnished by nature with a capacity for receiving them and are perfected in them through custom." (Aristotle, circa 340 B.C.) But there is also an appeal to reason, "... but, to those who form their desires and act in accordance with reason, to have knowledge on these points must be very profitable." (Aristotle, circa 340 B.C.) Specifically, Aristotle seems to look to government to provide the example, "Now the notions of nobleness and justice, with the examination of which politikea is concerned ..." (Aristotle, circa 340 B.C.).

In summary, Aristotle acknowledges a common understanding for right and wrong through reason which is assumed to be the bridge to happiness.[24] He also seems to take a modern viewpoint that right actions

principles first and then "happiness" (actually daily provision given the context) will follow; "But seek first the kingdom of God and his righteousness and all these things will be added to you." (ESV) Note Aristotle's attempt to emulate this Biblical truth that "all these things will be added"; "Now to be sure, if anything else is a gift of the Gods to men, it is probable that Happiness is a gift of theirs too, and specially because of all human goods it is the highest." (Aristotle, circa 340 B.C.)

[24] We could argue that Aristotle uses "borrowed capital" here, which means (as we have already stated) acknowledging a basis for right and wrong (see Romans 1:20, "... his eternal power and divine nature, have been clearly perceived ever since the creation of the world ..."), or "natural law," without giving God credit for it. For example, see this statement by Aristotle (circa 340 B.C.), "[happiness] ... not being sent from the Gods direct, but coming to us by reason of virtue and learning of a certain kind, or discipline, it is yet one of the most Godlike things; because the prize and End of virtue is manifestly somewhat most excellent, nay divine and blessed." He continues, "Further, that this aiming at the End is not a matter of one's own choice, but one must be born with a power of mental vision, so to speak, whereby to judge fairly and choose that which is really good; and he is blessed by nature who has this naturally well ..." (Aristotle, circa 340 B.C.).

are "discovered" through observation, or we could say through the "scientific method," so there is no acknowledgement of revelation from God as a basis for right and wrong.[25] He asks the question, "Are different individual things called good by virtue of being from one source, or all conducting to one end ..." (Aristotle, circa 340 B.C.). Aristotle does not want to discuss that there is a God who provides unity and answers his question, "... for even if there is some one good predicated in common of all things that are good, ... it cannot be the object of human action or attainable by Man."[26] (Aristotle, circa 340 B.C.) In fact, he ridicules any notion that standards do come from God, "... all praise does, as we have said, imply reference to a standard ... and this is illustrated by attempts to praise the gods; for they are presented in a ludicrous aspect by being referred to as our standard ..." (Aristotle, circa 340 B.C.). Aristotle does acknowledge that people have an inherent ethics problem, but since he does not see it as sin, can present no rational basis for overcoming this sin, "... we praise the Reason or Rational part of the Soul, because it exhorts aright and to the best course: but clearly there is in them, beside the Reason, some other natural principle which fights with and strains against the Reason." (circa 340 B.C.) So, the mind ("Reason") is certainly the battle-ground of morality, but "Reason" without Christ simply leads to mischief.[27] Let's now examine Aristotle's basis for moral application, "the golden mean."

The "Doctrine of the Mean" (or "Golden Mean") describes Aristotle's way of applying ethics to situations, "... rightness always means adaptation or adjustment to the special requirements of a

---

[25] Aristotle (circa 340 B.C.) states "... whether the right road is from principles or to principles ... Of course, we must begin with what is known; ..."

[26] This seems to reflect Kant's "noumenal" world that is "beyond our understanding" so not worth trying to explain so we need to "observe" the "phenomena" (particular actions that we see around us) and make conclusions from these observation (the basis of modernism and the scientific method for understanding the world).

[27] See Romans 7:22-23, "For I delight in the law of God, in my inner being, but I see in my members another law waging war against the law of my mind and making me captive to the law of sin that dwells in my members." (ESV)

situation. ..." (Aristotle, circa 340 B.C.) not too much or too little. This concept somewhat reflects Sproul's' "razor's edge" (see chapter 5 of this book), the difference being that Sproul looks to special revelation (the Scriptures) for the standard and Aristotle's standard ("Moral Sense") is somewhat vague:

> Now the Moral Virtue is a mean state, and how it is so, and that it lies between two faulty states, one in the way of excess and another in the way of defect, ... Then, again, he who makes a small deflection from what is right, be it on the side of too much or too little is not blamed, only he who makes a considerable one ... such questions [as to "point or degree a man must err to incur blame ..."] ... the decision of them rests with the Moral Sense. (Aristotle, circa 340 B.C.) (brackets added)

Let's look at one example of how Aristotle applies the "golden mean" to an issue we discussed earlier in the book and that is our attitude towards money.

> As for the life of money-making, it is one of constraint ... In respect of giving and taking wealth (a): The mean state is Liberality, the excess Prodigality, the defect Stinginess: ... the prodigal gives out too much and takes in too little, while the stingy man takes in too much and gives out too little. (Aristotle, circa 340 B.C.)

Aristotle creates lists of virtues and vices which reflect Scripture (righteousness and sin).[28] So there is a basis for a "code of conduct" in organizations of the right thing to do and the wrong thing. However, Aristotle tends to focus on inner qualities (i.e. "generosity") versus specific actions. For Aristotle, the most important quality is Justice or

---

[28] See Galatians 5:19-23 and James 3:13-18, for example.

"the just Man" but, "Coercion and ignorance of relevant circumstances render acts involuntary and exempt their doer from responsibility ..." (Aristotle, circa 340 B.C.).

Virtue theory seems to be closest (as compared to other secular views in this section) to the Biblical worldview, because it does seem to appeal indirectly to Natural Law. However, even though Aristotle seems to argue for a relationship between virtue and happiness, there doesn't seem to be a logical basis for the assertion. Aristotle himself points out weaknesses of virtue theory:

> We are right then in saying, that these virtues are formed in a man by his doing the actions; but no one, if he should leave them undone, would be even in the way to become a good man. Yes people in general do not perform these actions, but taking refuge in talk flatter themselves they are philosophizing, and that they will so be good men: acting in truth very like those sick people who listen to the doctor with great attention but do nothing that he tells them: just as these then cannot be well bodily under such a course of treatment, so neither can those be mentally by such philosophizing. (Aristotle, circa 340 B.C.)

The Christian worldview acknowledges that people in and of themselves do not have the will or power to do the right thing because of sin.[29] But, people are not as bad as they could be overall because of the presence of the Holy Spirit in the world (see chapter 5).

There is also a problem with who "gets the ball rolling." In other words, who sets the example of virtue that others need to follow? As mentioned previously, Aristotle looks to government to set this example:

---

[29] See Romans 3:9-12 as it quotes Psalm 14:1-3, "... For we have already charged that all, both Jews and Greeks, are under sin, as is written: 'None is righteous, no, not one; no one understands; no one seeks for God. All have turned aside; together they have become worthless; no one does good, not even one.'" (ESV)

> ... what takes place in communities: because the law-givers
> make the individual members good men by habituation,
> and this is the intention certainly of every law-giver, and all
> who do not effect it will fail of their own intent; and herein
> consists the difference between a good Constitution and a
> bad. (Aristotle, circa 340 B.C.)

In the 21st century, it is hard to imagine any government setting an example worth emulating for the rest of us!

Also, it is a little vague in virtue theory as to whether virtue is simply a label placed on an individual based on how the community perceives them or actual good done. "Since then the virtues are neither Feelings nor Capacities, it remains that they must be States. ... Virtue must be a state whereby Man comes to be good and whereby he will perform well his proper work." (Aristotle, circa 340 B.C.) This last sentence seems to be a circular statement. "Man comes to be good" so "he will perform well." But how does he "come to be good"? And is the "State" simply an impression about an individual by the community? How does that make them "good"?

Finally, virtue theory is fuzzy on the notion of personal responsibility. Aristotle, states, "Involuntary actions then are thought to be of two kinds, being done either on compulsion, or by reason of ignorance." (Aristotle, circa 340 B.C.) However, "ignorance" can also be classified as a sin of "omission"; something someone should do but has failed to do. And the Scripture argues that "ignorance" can be due to sin; "For although they knew God, they did not honor him as God or give thanks to him, but they became futile [ignorant] in their thinking, and their foolish hearts were darkened." (Romans 1:21, ESV) (brackets added) However, Aristotle (circa 340 B.C.) does clarify that some actions that may appear to be "by reason of ignorance" are actually done willfully, and the individual should be held accountable.

> And what makes the case stronger is this: that they chastise for
> the very fact of ignorance, when it is self-caused; to the drunken,

for instance, penalties are double, because the origination in such case lies in a man's own self: for he might have helped getting drunk, and this is the cause of his ignorance.

As this example points out, Aristotle does a good job of addressing potential misuses of his ideas and trying to clarify. Hence, his ideas have had much impact on Western civilization. Organizations can certainly benefit from Aristotle's notions (although more clearly articulated in Scripture) of mentoring to develop people, the importance of community (organizational culture) in setting out standards, and the desire for virtuous character qualities and habits.

Now let's look at a couple of others views that seem to have a broader use in current culture and business.

The Secular Humanist View

A basic view that still holds influence is the secular humanist view. This view has relatively long-standing roots and is summarized by a group of 34 humanists from 1933 (*Humanist Manifesto I*) and 40 years later by over 114 others (*Humanist Manifesto II*). The firm belief of the humanists is that Christianity (in particular) and all other religions (at least those that appeal to God for help and an external standard of morality) are not just irrelevant, but bad for culture and, in our case, bad for business. Historical religion should therefore be separated from any contact with worldly affairs, particularly the business world. In fact, the humanists go further by injecting the word *religion* with new meaning:

> There is a great danger of a final, and we believe fatal, identification of the word *religion* with doctrines and methods which have lost their significance and which are powerless to solve the problem of human living in The Twentieth Century. ... Today's man's larger understanding of the universe, his scientific achievements, and his deeper appreciation of brotherhood, have created a situation which

requires a new statement of the means and purposes of religion. (Kurtz, 1973, pp. 7-8)

Humanist Manifesto II (Kurtz, 1973) goes on to say:

> As in 1933, humanists still believe that traditional theism, especially faith in the prayer-hearing God, assumed to love and care for persons, to hear and understand their prayers, and to be able to do something about them, is an unproved and outmoded faith. Salvationism, based on mere affirmation, still appears as harmful, diverting people with false hopes of heaven hereafter. Reasonable minds look to other means for survival. (p. 13)

The authors then tie their movement to historical Marxism and define the basis for their "ethics":

> Many kinds of humanism exist in the contemporary world. The varieties and emphases of naturalistic humanism include "scientific," "ethical", "democratic", "religious", and "Marxist" humanism. ... Humanism is an ethical process through which we call can move, above and beyond the divisive particulars, heroic personalities, dogmatic creeds, and ritual customs of past religions or their mere negation. (Kurtz, 1973, p. 15)[30]

The Manifesto (I) goes on to list fifteen statements that redefine the word *religion*. For example, they appeal to an evolutionary view of mankind that emanates from their naturalistic worldview. This is important for our understanding of the terms used in business ethics. Most people are confused about what the terms really mean (see chapter

---

[30] Note the use of long quotes here to present this view. As stated at the beginning of the book, the author is not neutral; so it is more intellectually honest to present different ideas in the proponents' own words.

1) because they are not clear about their own worldview. Based on the humanistic view, the words can become meaningless; each person injecting their own definitions into the terms as truth evolves. It is important to identify the humanistic/naturalistic worldview when it comes to business ethics.

Let's take a closer look at a variation/application of this belief system: historic Marxism; also called (in its varied forms) Communism, Collectivism, Leftism or Progressivism. It is beyond the scope of this book to give a complete review of this ideology, but useful to examine a few basic tenets of the belief system and techniques that are still very much in use in culture and business.

Marxism is primarily a social/economic philosophy that opposes private property and holds that private business is fundamentally flawed as it (they would argue) concentrates wealth in the hands of a few and that leads to exploitation of workers[31] and resulting alienation of these workers.[32] They further see private business as a threat to governments in that they try to control governments so that they can take natural resources for their own and want to maintain the status quo so that their own interests will be protected. Marxists see happiness in terms of wealth; they who have wealth are happy and those who do not have wealth cannot be happy.[33] A utopia[34] can be achieved without God,

---

[31] Business leaders make workers labor hard under difficult conditions with very little pay while they reap huge profits.

[32] Workers see themselves more as things rather than people because of the way they are treated.

[33] The Scriptures certainly talk about fairness and justice but do not equate wealth with happiness and peace. In fact, Paul says just the opposite; that wealth (or lack thereof) should have no impact on our peace of mind (as we discussed in chapter 3): "... for I have learned in whatever situation I am to be content. I know how to be brought low, and I know how to abound. In any and every circumstance, I have learned the secret of facing plenty and hunger ... I can do all things through him who strengthens me." (Philippians 4:11-13, ESV)

[34] However, in today's application of Marxism, there seems to be no rational reason for believing that any "utopia" is being formed (see North Korea, Cuba et al.) So we could say that modern Marxism is simply nihilistic; wanting to destroy the current status quo, but solely for the purpose of securing power over others, not

when wealth is transferred and equality achieved. People are divided into groups, those who control natural resources are the "bourgeoisie" (private business in 21st century terms) and everyone else are the "proletariat" (workers) … and those groups should be in conflict.

Marxism was born out of a (rightful) concern for the excesses of the industrial revolution (late 1700s and 1800s) where workers were exploited.[35] However, Marxist ideology has a fatal flaw when it comes to ethics. Marxism uses ethical standards such as justice and fairness in its emotional appeal, yet shows no real rational basis for ethics in its ideology.[36] Engels (a colleague of Marx who helped frame the ideology)[37] describes morality as relative to the group who holds power and whose purpose is to simply further their economic aspirations.[38] This leads to a jaundiced view of ethics in general, thus providing no unchanging standard for the "rule of Law" in society, so "might makes right"; in other words, whoever has the (economic) power makes the rules.[39] This

---

really for doing anything for "the masses." But, it is far beyond the scope of this book to discuss this in more detail.

[35] We could say that Marxism is a Christian heresy, because it draws from powerful Biblical concepts of justice and concern for the poor (see chapter 7 of this book), yet has no basis for ethics on its own. So Marxism, is parasitical in that it draws from ethical consensus (particularly Christian) in culture and uses this good will to destroy culture.

[36] See quote in introduction of article (in *Marx-Engels Reader*) by Engels on morality: "… they [Marx and Engels] not only analyze exploitation and the division of labor in society, but morally condemn these phenomena as evil. Yet, there is almost no abstract discussion of ethics in their voluminous writings." (Tucker, 1978) (brackets added)

[37] Out of all the material written by Marx and Engels, this short article by Engels appears to be the only article related to ethics.

[38] See Engels' quote in the article entitled *On Morality*: "… men, consciously or unconsciously, derive their ethical ideas in the last resort from the practical relations on which their class position is based - from the economic relations in which they carry on production and exchange." (Tucker, 1978)

[39] "We therefore reject every attempt to impose on us any moral dogma whatsoever as an eternal, ultimate and forever immutable ethical law on the pretext that the moral world, too, has its permanent principles which stand above history and the differences between nations. We maintain on the contrary that all moral

leads to a focus on conflict to change the status quo. Marxism requires a fervent belief in the "utopia" and the government as the institution to administer "redemption" (Sproul, 1993).[40]

An example might help illustrate this point from the political realm. In the American political system (from its inception), the Rule of Law (the basis on which judges make legal decisions) has appealed to universal standards of Truth that don't change. If the humanist (Marxist) view is applied to the Rule of Law (which it has in many parts of the country), then judicial decisions are made based on partisan political concerns rather than eternal, unchanging standards. This results in the judiciary usurping the role of Congress by creating law by evolving their interpretations. Thus the Rule of Law becomes worthless. You can see the problem with a naturalistic and evolutionary view of law. The judicial system becomes a raw struggle for power. Respect for the law is lost because the law has no meaning except to further political purposes. What is particularly insidious about the humanistic approach is that those who practice such an approach take advantage of people by using familiar terms, but with different meanings. This technique can easily cause confusion. For those who theoretically think humanity is the highest good, this is a poor way to treat other people. It can easily lead to elitism under the guise of "helping the little guy."[41]

---

theories have been hitherto the product, in the last analysis, of the economic conditions of society obtained at the time. And as society has hitherto moved in class antagonisms, morality has always been class morality; it has either justified the domination and the interests of the ruling class, or, ever since the oppressed class became powerful enough, it has represented its indignation against this domination and the future interests of the oppressed." (Tucker, 1978)

[40] Contrast with the Biblical focus on God as our agent in redemption: "Put not your trust in princes, in a son of man, in whom there is no salvation. When his breath departs, he returns to the earth; on that very day his plans perish. Blessed is he whose help is the God of Jacob, whose hope is in the LORD his God, who made heaven and earth, the sea, and all that is in them, ..." (Psalms 146:3-6, ESV) and "The LORD will reign forever, your God, O Zion, to all generations." (Psalms 146:10, ESV)

[41] See discussion of Gnosticism later in this book.

So what does all of this have to do with business ethics? Let's briefly examine Marxist techniques and then look at practical implications. Conflict is fundamental to change in Marxist ideology.[42] Armed conflict is an option, but when the "proletariat" lacks power, then words become the vehicle for injecting conflict via the *polemic*. The polemic is simply verbal attacking. Its purpose is to seize the basis for discussion (the topic that is being discussed) and put opponents on the defensive. The goal is to use the opponent's own beliefs against them[43] so that your agenda is advanced and the opponent's is weakened. It is designed to get people to back off of their beliefs and to marginalize them.

This dynamic is not uncommon in business. Think about the times you have been yelled at aggressively by a superior or even another co-worker and how it makes you tend to acquiesce.[44] The polemic is "bullying with words."[45] When the polemic is involved, there is no basis for an open discussion to seek common ground. So "compromise" only means that you give up your beliefs.[46] This is why it is so important that you clearly understand your own ethics in business; so that you

---

[42] "But if the designing of the future and proclamation of ready-made solutions for all time is not our affair, then we realize all the more clearly what we have to accomplish in the present - *I am speaking of a ruthless criticism of everything existing*, ... the criticism must not be afraid of its own conclusions, nor of *conflict with the powers that be*." (Marx, 1844) (emphasis added)

[43] For example, this might involve attacking Christianity because one individual (i.e. a pastor caught doing drugs) fails to live up to Biblical standards. However, we know that a bad example doesn't mean the standard is wrong. Also Christians still sin, no one is perfect, which is why we need the grace of God daily.

[44] A corollary of the polemic is redefining your opponent's belief; for example asserting what "Christianity" teaches in terms that contradict the Bible or asserting "what the American people believe"; then marginalizing those who hold to the Biblical view or who disagree with the "popular" (which is in truth only asserted as such) view.

[45] Obviously, not everyone who uses the polemic embraces a Marxist ideology (worldview), but we could argue that the technique is Marxist.

[46] Keep in mind that there certainly are times to speak up strongly. Jesus confronted the Pharisees (see Matthew 23). But Jesus' confrontation was based on eternal Truth, not to coerce or manipulate.

will not abandon them when confronted strongly.[47] The goal is to stand your ground so that you can hopefully have a discussion on what is important with others.[48]

Situation Ethics

Another more current approach is *situation* ethics, which we could argue is the modern application of aspects of utilitarianism and deontology. Situation ethics was developed by Joseph Fletcher, an Episcopalian priest, in the early 1960s to try to avoid what he saw as the extremes of legalism (doing more than the law requires resulting in being judgmental) and antinomianism (*against law* or falling short of what the law requires, being too loose). He proposed that the only absolute is *love* and each person determines what this is in any situation. He "took" his system from 1 John 4:8 in the Bible where it says: "He who does not love does not know God, for God is love." He developed his ideas during the turmoil of the 1960s in the United States where all conventions in society were questioned. Some say that Fletcher developed an ethical system that suited the behavior of the 60s, so that people could maintain a lifestyle contrary to historic Christianity and feel good about it. For example, it is possible that Fletcher may have inspired the Beatles hit song from the 60s "All You Need is Love."

According to Fletcher, we are to keep in mind rules (or *guidelines* as they are called) and traditions as we face ethical decisions but should feel free to override them in the name of *love*. If you have a motive of love then the end justifies the means you use to show love in a certain situation. Fletcher, in his writing, gives some criteria to follow to determine how to help the person whose need is greater: (1) perform the action that helps the greatest number; (2) help the person who is

---

[47] See Ephesians 6:10-20, especially verse 13: "Therefore take up the whole armor of God, that you may be able to withstand in the evil day, and having done all, to stand firm." (ESV)

[48] Organizations can also face this belief system when it comes to Corporate Social Responsibility (CSR) issues (see chapter 7 of this book).

more valuable. Two other principles advocated by Fletcher include: the removal of antithesis (so no clear cut distinction between and right and wrong in any situation so the meaning of the word *love* is not clear cut in all situations); and avoiding absolute terms such as *no, always, don't.*

How would situation ethics work in social situations? Fletcher in his book *Situation Ethics* (1966) presented a number of examples to back up his idea to show that sometime it is more loving to go against accepted standards. For example, an imprisoned woman in an occupied country who agreed to have relations with a guard to escape and help her family would be seen as moral. This and other difficult situations show that many times love demands that accepted standards need to be violated. If you really care, and that drives your decision, then you have done the right thing. But you should never strive to take your choices and develop rules or standards that might apply to others in other situations. Each situation is unique.

The hit television series *24* was replete with examples of Situation Ethics. For example, should a loving husband and father kill a weapons supplier because he needs to obtain a part and deliver it to a terrorist in order to save his family (Season 6)? The example illustrates one of the problems with Situation Ethics. Is there any guarantee that the terrorist will keep his word and not kill the family anyway (which happened)? Also, is the part that the man killed to obtain really a critical component needed to detonate a nuclear device that would eventually kill the family and thousands of others in the area (which it was)? In other words in situation ethics (and also utilitarianism as we discussed previously), it is very difficult to take into account all of the factors that go into evaluating a situation accurately.

Tonya Harding thought she could advance her figure skating career by getting some help from some close friends. On January 6, 1994, Harding's closest competitor for the U.S. Olympic Skating Team and potential Olympic gold metal was attacked. Some mysterious individuals entered the Detroit skating arena where Nancy Kerrigan was working out and proceeded to hit her on the outside of her right knee. After an investigation, Harding's ex-husband (Jeff Gillooly) was charged with conspiring to arrange the attack. The United States Figure Skating Association (USFSA) later accused Harding of participating in the scheme and took away her 1994 National Championship and banned her for life. Undaunted, posted on Harding's website was the following claim:

> For good, for bad, depending on your point of view, Tonya Harding has been one of the most influential or perhaps controversial persons in Figure Skating history, and in all sports history, in notoriety, perhaps second only to Mohammad Ali. ... her website is dedicated to her desires and dreams. ... Tonya remains a figure people wish to know more about, even if it's idle curiosity.

Some say that Gillooly's motive for carrying out the crime was "love" for his ex-wife and a desire to "win" her back by "proving" himself by helping her achieve her goals. This shows a potential problem with Situation Ethics, the means for helping can become fuzzy.

We have just covered some examples of ethical systems. Obviously, there are others. For example, we haven't looked at the views of different religions (such as Judaism, Hinduism, Buddhism, Islam and others) which are important to determine, for example, when doing business in foreign cultures.

FINDING COMMON STANDARDS

We need to consider the "ethics of others" to work in a diverse organizational environment. However, that doesn't mean that you have to give up your own ethics. It also doesn't mean that there has to be chaos, with happens when people assert their own standards based on power and manipulation. There is a slogan that appears on U.S. money that reads: "e pluribus Unum," which means "out of the many, one." Historically, this has been the culture of the U.S.A.; to welcome people from all over the world ("many") and unite them ("one") around the Constitution and a common love for freedom and clear and consistent application of the law (based on Natural Law). It highlights the importance (not only in countries, but also in companies) of finding a point of unity amidst the diversity. Let's briefly explore how we can find a common standard and apply it in business and even culture.

In his book *Mere Christianity*, C.S. Lewis summarizes his talks given on the radio (at the bequest of the British Broadcasting Corporation, or BBC) in Great Britain during World War II. Because of his previous work on pain and suffering, the radio station thought that he might be able to provide comfort to the British peoples during these difficult times; so he was asked by the BBC to do a series on what Christians believe. Apparently he did give comfort or at least evoke interest, as his radio presentations were widely popular. In this challenging context of bullets and bombs, Lewis began his presentations by discussing Right and Wrong as a Clue to the Meaning of the Universe. It is interesting that his focus was not on sympathy but on ethics. Because his words were given (and well received) by real people (not just academicians) in the worst possible situation (war and invasion facing the British people), they are particularly useful in our analysis of the meaning of the term ethics and ramifications for business ethics (finding a common ground amidst diversity).

Lewis (1952) begins his argument by reminding us that we often quarrel because we think others have not pleased us. So, if we insist that a friend has not pleased us, then we must be appealing to some standard by which we measure the other's behavior; and based on our measurement, the behavior falls short. Now when you tell your friend his problem, he often reacts by saying that he has not wronged you. He is fully in line with his own standards, which unfortunately do not align with yours. Voila! … the root of conflict.

Lewis (1952) continues by pointing out that this standard to which we all appeal is referred to as the Law of Nature (we might clarify by saying the Law of *Human* Nature or *Moral Law* or *Natural Law*). It was the law of decent behavior that everyone knew by nature and did not need to be taught. Just as the physical world is held to laws, so humanity is held to laws. And just like in the law of gravity, you are certainly free to violate the law by jumping out of a very tall building, you are free to violate the Law of Human Nature. However, just like the law of gravity, if you violate the law you will find out that things will not go well for you. Because for example, even though you are "free" to jump out of a very tall building, you will quickly face the reality that indeed the law of gravity does apply and you will probably end up as a very flat and dead individual. Lewis argues, based on extensive research summarized in his book the *Abolition of Man*, that this Law of Human Nature is common throughout history and across cultures. For example he says that a man who does not believe in right and wrong (or making promises that you keep) will complain bitterly the moment you break a promise **to him.**

The rest of the book is very instructive, but the point for our purposes is that we could argue (as Lewis and others have) that there is a common standard of living to which all of us can appeal that is universal (**Theistic** view). This Law of Human Nature (or Natural Law) of which Lewis reminds us was historically (in western civilization) the standard to which the word ethics appealed. So as we think of business ethics and setting up ethical standards for our businesses, we can set standards that are good and true; **no matter where the business is located**. It is not just a relativistic pursuit.

Friedman (1962) concurs. He emphasizes a need for a common ethic: "Voluntary cooperation vs. totalitarianism based on a common ethic" (p. 13). Friedman (1962) cites the role of government as, like an umpire, upholding common standards (p. 25). As he puts it:

> Men's freedoms can conflict, and when they do, one man's freedom must be limited to preserve another's ... The major problem in deciding the appropriate activities of government is how to resolve such conflicts among the freedoms of different individuals. (Friedman, 1962, p. 26)

One standard has to serve as the basis from which each individual pursues his or her own freedom. As mentioned above, historically, this has been the Theistic view in United States government and business.

Ford (2003) highlights this common ground needed for carrying out any group endeavor. His comments apply to government, but the same principle applies to business. We need a common ethical standard for carrying out business:

> ... they also soon embraced the idea of such a [covenantal] fidelity in all their societal obligations. Any human relation [such as business] that demanded virtue was seen as requiring such a godly frame. According to the covenantal model, all societies must derive their virtues from among their members, conforming themselves to the will of God. The mutual observance of God's moral code would itself provide the means of their common virtue. Those ruling from above would be in service ... to the moral code ... Less civil regulation would be necessary .... (p. 125)[49] (brackets added)

Ford assumes a Theistic standard (reflecting the original founders of the United States of America) but the point for our purposes is that businesses must articulate a common organizational standard for ethics, whatever that standard might be.

There is a pressing need in business to make sure that we get business ethics right. There is too much at stake. Because, as we have stated throughout the book, those who conduct their business in an ethical manner will do well **in the long run**. This truth applies to individuals working in business who set standards for themselves and also to leaders of organizations who set up standards for all the people in their organizations.

For example, Adam Smith points to the importance of ethics for capitalism to work. Bradley mentions that Adam Smith (1723-1790)

---

[49] We discussed in detail this covenantal concept in chapter 3 of this book.

was the Professor of Moral Philosophy of the University of Glasgow. Bradley (2003) comments on Smith:

> Smith identified two roads to worldly status. One was paved by the "study of wisdom and the practice of virtue;" the other by "the acquisition of wealth and greatness" for their own sake. Wisdom and virtue was the high road from which the best could be expected; the latter, which Smith denigrated as 'proud ambition and ostentatious avidity,' was a path wrought with deceit and ruin. What was true in Smith's day will be found to be equally true in ours. (pp. 5-6)

One of my good friends (Hagerman) who has worked successfully in business for over 30 years in a number of different capacities, but primarily in improving operations through coaching key leaders, independently endorses Smith's point of view. He says this: "ethical leaders want to DO something great with others" (reflection of Smith's study of wisdom and the practice of virtue as motive). They work hard by taking action to do the right thing for the business and the people in that business. My friend then states, "unethical people tend to want to BE someone important" (reflection of Smith's acquisition of wealth and greatness as motive). They are only concerned about their own status. They focus their energies in a political way to further their own position.

The point is that Adam Smith never assumed a capitalistic system with morality out of control. He assumed that ethics was the foundation of his economic system. If you remove this important worldview assumption, then of course you have all kinds of abuses. To answer the critics of capitalism, when companies violate ethical standards, they are usually known (and rightly so) for violating those prescribed standards. They are held accountable. Political capitalists, on the other hand, have no rational basis for acting ethically so focus on form rather than substance. Bradley (2003) sums it up:

A truer understanding of Adam Smith casts a decidedly different light on recent controversies [referring to Enron and other business problems in the early 2000s]. Smith's major ideas, while certainly tested, still hold force. Capitalism has a moral dimension from which participants can be praised or criticized—and prosecuted in the event of force or fraud. Good will ultimately prevail over bad given the operation of the laws of justice and "the obvious and simple system of natural liberty." Political capitalists should be viewed with the greatest of suspicion. And nominally altruistic behavior in the marketplace should be judged in light of deeper motivations and results, not only public relations. (p. 11) (brackets added)

Businesses should not shy away from appealing to universal standards in setting up and applying their business ethics. There is a political and economic precedent for this appeal. Let's look in more detail at exactly how this should and shouldn't work.

INTEGRATION ISSUES

Now, we need to understand ethical integration issues in business. In other words, we want to explore issues/solutions as we interact with the ethics of others and the ethics of the organization in finding "a common ground for doing business" (see Ruddell's model from chapter 1 of this book). As we live out our ethics, it is easy to lose track of our standards due to the many influences from others, government and culture. Again, I am using the Christian point of view as my foundation.

Richard Niebuhr (1975) adds to our discussion in his important analysis of how Christianity (or faith in general) and culture interact. **All** people do something with this dynamic of how faith and culture (in our case business) interact. Even ignoring the relationship is in itself a reaction. As we consider a faith-based approach to business ethics, it is important to examine Niebuhr's ideas. However, my purpose is not to present his material in completion. I am taking some of his ideas and applying them particularly to the business environment. So, I have taken the liberty to apply some of his views from a different perspective.

Niebuhr (1975) presents five ways for how Christianity and culture can interact. For our purposes, only four are pertinent to business ethics. The four that we will look at are (to make it clearer, I include the word *business* because we are talking particularly about organizational culture, including business ethics):

- Christ Against Business Culture
- Christ Of Business Culture
- Christ Above Business Culture
- Christ the Transformer of Business Culture

Let me briefly comment on how I take these four categories in regards to business ethics (to look at Niebuhr's original ideas, I invite you to read his original material. In several cases, I apply different meanings to his original ideas). *Christ Against Business Culture* (looking at it in a way slightly differently from Niebuhr's view) suggests that Christ (or faith) is bad for business. Theistic faith is not neutral but, in the opinion of the humanist, destructive to the work environment: "We believe, however, that traditional dogmatic or authoritarian religions that place revelation, God, ritual, or creed above human needs and experiences do a disservice to the human species" (Kurtz, 1973, pp. 15-16). So, this view does not tolerate any expressions of faith in the work place. *Business is business*, so there is no room for "religion." Either it will make you too nice and naive so that you can't compete effectively or it will make you too legalistic and judgmental towards others. You can't force your views on others. However, as we have already discussed, everyone has a "religion" (something they believe in to make life work) so this view simply wants to assert one belief system over the other.

I saw an example of this in one of my consulting situations. A young lady (from my organization) arrived from out of town to work on a project with our team for several months. She was undoubtedly a Christian. To encourage herself (and others who cared to look), she wrote a scripture each week on the white board in her cubicle. After several weeks, she was called into our manager's office and warned that she shouldn't do that; it was *harmful* to others. The manager wanted us to remain neutral. My point is that this manager was not being *neutral*. He had taken the view that Christianity was bad for culture; it was *against* what we are trying to accomplish. He had an agenda, though not articulated.

The next category is *Christ of Business Culture*. I take this to mean (similar to Niebuhr) that individuals in business state a Christian belief but their modus operandi is *business is business*. They see themselves as spiritual people wanting to do good. They think that because they have such good intentions, they must be holy and acceptable. What indeed happens is that they bring Christ and His standards down to their level. They adjust the standard to fit what they are doing so that they can still consider themselves as *good Christian people*. I think this view leads to the error of antinomianism,[50] going against the Law and breaking what the Law requires.

The business leader articulates a faith, may attend church, may read the Bible, may quote verses and may help the community; but when it comes to carrying out the business, he lives by the motto: *business is business*. The person who holds this Christ of Business Culture view would probably not ask the young lady to remove the verses from the white board, but he wouldn't read them or apply them. Ken Lay is a good example of this view. He attended church and did many good things for the city of Houston during his leadership of Enron. But the internal business activities of Enron, as we have discovered, were unethical. Yet, I am sure he (and others concurred) considered himself a good Christian. Now don't get me wrong, I am not denying that Lay might have a genuine faith. But if he does, it did not seem to impact, in a real way, his business decisions (or lack thereof) at Enron.

---

[50] We will discuss antinomianism in chapter 5 of this book.

A good friend of mine faced a difficult situation. He entered into a business agreement with another Christian man who agreed to share the cost of a large piece of equipment that would benefit both of their businesses. The partner made full use of the equipment but never paid a cent for it. My friend was stuck with the entire cost, which almost broke his business. But instead of suing, he faithfully paid it off. The partner claimed to be a Christian with his lips but when it came to money, his attitude was *business is business*. Apparently he lowered Christ and redefined His standards to allow for this seemingly unethical behavior in order to call it OK.

The Christ of Culture view reflects a Gnostic approach to business ethics. The Gnostics (ancient philosophy from Biblical times) believed that the body was evil and the spirit was good. So, as long as you had the right insight or knowledge (*gnosis*) spiritually, you were OK. This resulted in a couple of approaches to dealing with the body. Some denied the body and ignored it. This was Stoicism, best illustrated in the movie *Gladiator*. Since the body was evil, it had to be aggressively controlled and denied, particularly regarding emotions. But this approach (though outwardly somewhat controlled) can lead to a lack of personhood and the carrying out of cold, hard abuses of others. The other reaction allowed by Gnosticism is Epicureanism, the pursuit of pleasure. Since true spirituality comes through proper understanding and the body doesn't matter, then indulgence is fine. You can pursue pleasure with your body (including greed and the benefits of greed) as long as you have the right spirituality. This idea is prominent in political circles where ethics is measured by having the right political view. Anything is allowed, as long you are correct on the proscribed political issues. This is also true in business. We have discussed previously the example from the film *Crimes and Misdemeanors* where the lead character gets away with murder (literally) yet continues to have his privileged world of respect, money, and devotion from his family as if nothing had changed. The main character made no admissions to a personal faith but his response is illustrative. He had adjusted his initial standards to fit his actions: Christ of Culture. Whenever we violate eternal standards

111

(as we have discussed), we always have two choices. We can say the standard is wrong because we are good people and wouldn't normally do such a thing so something must be wrong with the standard. Or, we can admit that the standard is correct and we are wrong and realize we must change to bring our own lives in line with the standard. The Christ of Culture view suggests the former approach.

I have spent more time on the first two views because I think they are most common today. Now let's examine the last two.

The *Christ Above Business Culture* approach says, in my opinion (somewhat different than Niebuhr), that as Christians we have to keep ourselves from being stained by the non-Christians in the world. We have to remove ourselves from them. We do not participate in parties, lunch with other employees, other corporate events, after-work get-togethers, or office break chatter. We are above or better than the others so we must remove ourselves. We sometimes lob a tract or other means of witnessing at our co-workers but we don't develop meaningful relationships with them as people. Leaders who hold this view may have Bible studies and other activities for workers but not relate with them in other ways. This approach can result in the creation of rules and regulations to guide employees in the proper way, which can be good. But, this view can also lead to Legalism (see chapter 5 of this book) which is adding to what the Law requires. Obviously this can slow down performance by sacrificing genuine productivity for bureaucracy. The process becomes the goal instead of the real and necessary business goals and strategies. Also creativity is minimized. Rigid guidelines are imposed from management so individuals are not free to improve upon current status quo.

I do concur with Niebuhr's view of *Christ the Transformer of Business Culture.* This view takes the stance that Christians (people of faith) are intimately involved with those in business but their distinctive Christian standards are not lost. They are actively practiced in real ways in real situations so that they have a positive impact. Through a model of hard work, treating people well, showing wisdom, showing fairness, and following the intent of the Law, this leader changes others. It is not coercive. It is not deceptive. It is real. It is genuine. This is the proper relationship between faith and business culture.

I was talking to a leader at a large international university about the consulting work he was doing with a small energy company. He was helping the company develop a business ethics statement. The statement was representative of many in business today. I then asked, "what is the philosophical foundation for those statements"? I wanted to understand what made those particular statements true and others not. He looked at me with a blank stare. He had no idea what I was talking about. This is typical in business ethics circles. We use the terms but do not know about their meanings.

So how do you stand up to the varied ethical approaches of others and organizations? The premise of this book is that everyone has a faith (belief) but most people don't realize what that faith is or don't realize that it is relevant in the business world. To say it another way, I want you to identify your faith (whatever it is) and knowingly apply it. So, what about you? What do you believe? I challenge you to think seriously about what you believe so that when you face those difficult situations, you will do the right thing instead of simply reacting to what everyone else does. I have made the statement, "The person who does not know what they believe, will under pressure do anything." It is imperative that you know yourself so you are true to yourself even in the midst of the worst circumstances. Don't lose yourself by being swallowed up by somebody else's ranting. Don't give up your freedom so easily. Maintain your humanity. Don't lose what makes you uniquely human. Take a stand today. Define your standards and remain true to them. Do it now.

CHAPTER 4 QUESTIONS FOR REVIEW

1. Explain Utilitarianism; its basic tenets, and how it compares/ contrasts with the Biblical worldview. Do you agree or disagree? Why?

2. Explain Deontology; its basic tenets, and how it compares/ contrasts with the Biblical worldview. Do you agree or disagree? Why?

3. Explain Virtue Theory; its basic tenets, and how it compares/ contrasts with the Biblical worldview. Do you agree or disagree? Why?

4. Explain the Secularistic Humanist View; its basic tenets, and how it compares/contrasts with the Biblical worldview. Do you agree or disagree? Why?

5. Explain Situation Ethics; its basic tenets, and how it compares/ contrasts with the Biblical worldview. Do you agree or disagree? Why?

6. Why do we need to consider "the ethics of others" as described in this chapter?

7. Review Ruddell's (derived from Niebuhr) four ways of explaining "integration" of your own ethics with the ethics of others. Analyze and give one or two examples of how you see them practiced in your current (or future) organization.

8. Based on material from this chapter (or the previous one), describe and analyze the belief system that serves as the foundation for your organization's culture.

9. Describe and analyze the belief systems of two or three people that you work with. Where can you find "a common ground for doing business" with these individuals based on your own standards?

10. Discuss how important it is to you that your organization's workplace values are in accordance with your own values. What are the dangers of a disconnect between workplace values and individual values?

Chapter

5

MAKE ETHICS WORK BY SOLVING ETHICAL PROBLEMS

THE PURPOSE OF THIS SECTION is to give you some application ideas and inspire you to use those ideas in your specific work situation. Keep in mind that I am using my Christian standards as the foundation for my applications. However, I think that you will find the issues raised in this chapter (and the next) beneficial no matter what your worldview. Let's start by looking at the two major applications of business ethics: solving ethical problems (covered in this chapter) and setting up and carrying out an effective ethics program[1] (covered in the next chapter).

IMPORTANCE OF SOLVING ETHICAL PROBLEMS

The application of the Christian model is important. It is not enough to have principles laid out neatly, you must apply those principles in real situations. In business, you must apply the principles in two important ways. First, you must understand and solve ethical problems that you face. This means that you must not only know your principles well (the focus of chapter 4 for the Christian point

---

[1]   Part of this second application can also include a program to reach out to those outside of the organization; called Corporate Social Responsibility (CSR), the subject of chapter 7 of this book.

115

of view), but you must also understand your business well. The better you know your business, the more likely you will clearly see when someone attempts to do the wrong thing. This was one of the problems at Enron. Enron was known for its innovation, receiving a number of awards for this quality. So, when things did not seem right in the business, many people probably thought something like this: "Oh well. This is a very innovative company. Our leaders must know what they are doing because of the many positive articles written about them. So, even though this seems funny, it must just be a new, creative way to do our business. I need to learn more before I can comment on it." It was more complex for some of the senior managers. For example, Sherron Watkins faced a quandary when she worked in commercial support with Enron's Caribbean operations (Schwartz with Watkins, 2003):

> In the last four months of 1999, in fact, Sherron's Caribbean tasks were increasingly focused on window-dressing Enron's financial statements. She sold Promigas, the Colombian natural gas pipeline, to a new off-balance sheet vehicle, Whitewing. The "sale" was in name only. Enron recorded the $136 million in cash from Whitewing as cash flow from operations, not as cash flow from money borrowed, which in reality was more like it. ... Moreover, Whitewing's off-balance sheet status seemed shaky. Whitewing (also known as Condor, its project name) featured an ownership chart involving more than twenty entities ... But the overall entity, Whitewing Associates LP, listed Enron as both the general and limited partner. It was close to impossible to tell whether enough outside ownership existed in Whitewing to legitimately qualify it as an off-balance-sheet SPE. (p. 181)

Sherron did question these activities. "But Sherron began to wonder just how many $100 million deals were designed to enhance the balance sheet in just that way" (Schwartz with Watkins, 2003, p. 181). However, it was hard to sort out the exact unethical behavior because of the innovation involved. Her initial recourse was to try to leave. "The thought occurred to Sherron that it might be time to look for a job outside Enron" (Schwartz with Watkins, 2003, p. 182). Sherron faced the difficult situation of realizing that there were questionable activities taking place, but not having the political power or interest to do much about it. Enron did not have a workable plan in place for dealing with ethical problems. This deficiency hurt Sherron and hurt the organization as well. Let's learn from this example.

It is important to develop an approach for solving ethical problems in your organization. There are a number of books[2] and articles on approaches to ethical decision making. This is important, especially in terms of compliance with the law.[3] The Scriptures suggest an approach to solving ethical problems with a focus on the people involved. This is instructive since all ethical problems occur because individuals (at

---

[2] Most books on business ethics contain a section or chapter on an approach to ethical decision making. For example, Cavanagh's book (1998) devotes most of chapter 3 (pages 73-91) to this topic; and *The Ethical Edge* (1995) lists its general approach for making decisions on pages 27-28 as part of what the authors call the *ethical point of view*.

[3] A company can reduce its culpability before the law when individuals in that company act unethically if they can demonstrate that they follow a standard approach to resolving ethical issues.

some level) are doing unethical things.[4] The Scriptures recommend a three-step approach to solving problems.[5]

1. Go to the person privately and point out their error based on organizational standards.
2. If the person does not listen, find one or two others to join you (as witnesses) and talk with the person again.

---

[4] This is where I would disagree that organizations per se are *guilty* and thus are liable to be accused like a person. Only individuals can truly be guilty so at some level you look for individual responsibility for a corporate problem. I have two concerns with this notion of calling the entire organization *guilty*. The first concern is that one of the reasons for this willingness to give *personal* responsibility to an organization is to allow people to make more money when they sue (a corporation has more money than an individual). Thus, the regular workers in the company often suffer the most when a company goes out of business (due to extreme amounts of settlement money), when perhaps the company leaders were the guilty ones and should be the ones suffering. My second concern, at a higher level, is that the capitalistic system itself is accused of *evil* (again giving the organization an ethical status as a human being) when individual leaders in a particular company act unethically. I do agree that organizations bear the ethical stamp of their key leaders (good or bad) but I disagree that this means that the system is bad. See my work on values in leadership and how those values affect organizational culture (Ruddell, 1993).

[5] See Matthew 18:15-17, "Moreover if your brother sins against you, go and tell him his fault between you and him alone. If he hears you, you have gained your brother. But if he will not hear, take with you one or two more, that 'by the mouth of two or three witnesses every word may be established.' And if he refuses to hear them, tell it to the church, let him be to you like a heathen and a tax collector." Also see the verses following this passage. In the context, it appears that the *church* as it is used here refers to the leaders of the church, not necessarily everyone in the church, although eventually you will want to inform everyone in the church of the action taken. See 2 Corinthians 2:5-7 where apparently all the members of the church in Corinth were aware of the punishment given to a wrong-doer so Paul asks for their help in encouraging him after he changed. A business organization is different from a church (step #3). So, the organization must decide who will handle step #3. I think an ethics commission should be established (which may or may not be part of the organization) made up of different groups of people, representing different perspectives of the company. However, members should be known for their ethical and fair and discerning behavior.

3. If the person does not listen the second time, bring them before the entire leadership team for the purpose of taking further action.

The majority of writing in business ethics focuses on the function of identifying and solving ethical problems. You might say (from a theological perspective) that this approach deals with sins of commission, solving problems caused by people doing the wrong thing. You do want to correct the things that people are doing wrong and manage the repercussions as smoothly as possible[6] for your organization.

Let's now explore how to discern problems and correct them. We have already discussed a basic approach for handling people as an example. Now let's explore this issue in more detail. As you apply your organization's ethical standards, you will find that some decisions will be very easy and others will be very complicated.[7] It helps to remember an important saying, that there is nothing new under the sun.[8] In other words, the patterns of unethical behavior will be the same as others have faced. The particulars will differ, but overall the issues are the same. In fact, the clearer you are with your ethical standards as an organization, the easier it will be to make some ethical decisions (but certainly not all). Many ethical decisions become difficult because those making the decisions are really looking for a way to get around the ethics altogether.[9] Now let's look at a more detailed approach for identifying and solving ethical problems that occur within organizations.

---

[6] We could say, this points to the risk management function of business ethics. You want to handle problems effectively not only to do the right thing but to limit your liability as an organization; and the reason you want to set up an ethics program is to prevent problems in the first place.

[7] Again, refer to Ruddell's model (chapter 1 of this book). When you are solving ethical problems in organizations, you need to refer to the organization's ethics as the standard. As long as your standards line up (for the most part) with those of the organization, then you will eliminate at least one potential cause of complication.

[8] See, for example, Ecclesiastes 1:9, "That which has been is what will be, That which is done is what will be done, *And there is nothing new under the sun.*" (emphasis added)

[9] See later in this chapter on "loopholism."

AN APPROACH FOR SOLVING ETHICAL ISSUES

Any approach for solving ethical issues seeks to apply ethical standards in an ethical way. I will seek to demonstrate this consistency as I lay out my approach. I will start by listing the steps that I recommend for ethical decision making:

1. Realize that an ethical standard has been violated
2. Identify all of the people affected by the ethical violation
3. Gather pertinent information from all concerned
4. Analyze all of the information, looking at all sides, according to your organizational standards
5. Make a decision based on your organizational standards, taking into consideration what is good for all the people who are affected by the decision including, as much as possible, the individual who acted unethically
6. Implement the decision ethically
7. Discuss the lessons learned from the situation and how to avoid the problem in the future without punishing all the people in the organization through excessive policies.

Let's look at each step in more detail and the ethical standards they represent. Some form of some of these general steps has been used by many so they are common knowledge.

Realize that an ethical standard has been violated

Become an expert about the business operations and the ethical standards of your organization. Be wise about people and what they are doing. You must be aware of how some have practiced unethical behaviors in the past in your type of organization so that you can discern if someone is doing the same thing currently. If people don't know the standard (see Ruddell's model from chapter 1, the organizational ethics circle), then people are not aware that an ethical violation has taken place.

Here, it is useful to name the unethical behavior; "that's lying, that's stealing, that is being deceptive" (for example). See the movie *Office Space* when the lead character tries to explain to his girl friend how he plans to move percentage points of pennies electronically from his company's transaction account to his own account and sees this as OK. After his explains, his girl friend says "that's stealing." The lead character then says "no, you don't understand ...." And then the girl friend perceptively asks, "so you're taking something, right? ... and it's not yours, right? ... how is that not stealing?"[10]

Leaders must live the organizational standards and communicate them to the rest of the organization through word and deed (this is the subject of chapter 6) so that everyone will recognize a violation of the standards when they occur. Otherwise, no one will take action to address the problem, which is an issue in many organizations.

Identify all of the people affected by the ethical violation

This step demonstrates an overall concern for people as well as making sure you have complete and accurate information. You want to consider all of the people (stakeholders) who are affected in some way by the ethical problem. It is important to identify these people so that you can communicate effectively with them about the problem and how you handle the problem.

Gather pertinent information from all concerned

After you acknowledge that there is a problem, you go about gathering information about the ethical violation, perhaps the most difficult step. The difficulty comes because the leaders of the organization have two roles to fulfill in respect to ethical issues. They have a legal role to fulfill

---

[10] See Genesis 3:8-11 where God uses questions to confront based on standards He had laid down; "'Where are you?'" (v. 9); "'Who told you that you were naked? Have you eaten of the tree of which I commanded you not to eat?'" (v. 11)

to uphold the law in their organization and they must manage the risk of potential litigation about the matter and the negative publicity that might result. The legal goal is to find and punish those who do harm to the organization. This is to protect the integrity of the organization so that those who act unethically, particularly leaders, will not pollute the rest of the organization. From a Christian theological point of view, we call this action of establishing and enforcing justice according to solid standards the *kingly* role of leadership.

Good leaders also have a concern for people so they want to treat people well in the process of gathering information. You want to develop people, which involves encouraging people instead of judging them (which is inferred in the legal approach). From a Christian theological point of view, we call this the *priestly* role of serving as a mediator by showing love and consideration to others.

When gathering information, it is important to take more of a priestly role and then let the data force you to take a kingly role when making a decision. One of the principles to guide you in this process is from Proverbs 18:17, "The first one to plead his cause seems right, Until his neighbor comes and examines him." It is important to hear from all sides on an ethical matter before passing judgment. Many times we hear the story from one person and we automatically jump to conclusions about another person. This is not a complete evaluation. We need to give the other person the chance to explain themselves, while verifying the data presented by the first person.

Another important principle is to gather only pertinent data from those concerned. There is no need to drag others into the investigation if they are not part of the situation. Also, it is important to keep the investigation as confidential as possible so as not to stir up rumors and gossip.

Gathering information should not be done, at least initially, using only a legal approach (although it depends on the severity of the issue!). You must treat each person as a human being. A person is presumed innocent until proven guilty. An honest person will normally not mind pointed, but fair questions, which can normally lead to a quick resolution and peace restored.

However, unethical people are more devious. So, whenever you find an unethical activity taking place, you almost always find someone lying to cover it up. It takes someone with discernment to be able to distinguish between the denials of an honest person and the denials of a lying person who is trying to cover up or shift the blame. That is why it is important to have people with strengths in discernment on the data gathering team.

So who should gather data? You can see that investigating an ethical issues is almost like playing the role of detective. Organizations should think through how they want to structure an investigative effort. In smaller companies, two or three people should be placed on a team to investigate, including questioning suspects.[11] In larger organizations, the investigative function can be out-sourced. In any case, this is going to be a cross-functional effort including (but not limited to) the legal department, the personnel department, the business ethics team, the accounting department (when finances are involved) and often the IT group (for misuse of the computer and/or phone).

One final point, it is important that you are diligent in gathering information.[12] Much harm can be done if you are not thorough in checking into **pertinent** matters related to the investigation.

Analyze all of the information, looking at all sides

When analyzing the information, it is important to avoid the extremes of legalism and antinomianism. This is Sproul's (1986) *razor's edge.*

---

[11] This is the Biblical approach (see earlier in chapter); "But if he does not listen, take one or two others along with you, that every charge may be established by the evidence of two or three witnesses." (Matthew 18:16, ESV)

[12] See 1 Corinthians 5:1-2 where Paul chides the Corinthian (church) organization for NOT being diligent in investigating an ethical issue (although we could also say this was a failure of Step 1, failing to recognize and take seriously the ethical standards); "It is actually reported that there is sexual immorality among you, and of a kind that is not tolerated even among pagans, for a man has his father's wife. And you are arrogant! Ought you not rather morn: Let him who has done this be removed from among you." (ESV)

> The continuum of ethics is divided sharply by a fine line, the razor's edge. This fine line of demarcation is similar to what Jesus described as the "narrow way." ... There is a difference between a narrow way and narrow-mindedness. Narrow-mindedness reveals a judgmental attitude, a critical mindset, which is far from the Biblical ideal of charity. Walking the narrow way involves not a distorted mental attitude, but a clear focus of what righteousness demands (p. 31).

This razor's edge denotes the distinction between justice and mercy. You must maintain a proper blend between both. To overdue the mix in either direction causes problems. The error resulting from an overemphasis on justice to the detriment of mercy is called legalism. This is going beyond what the law requires. The error resulting from overemphasis on mercy to the detriment of justice is called antinomianism (antilawism ... libertinism ... the Christian falls short of obeying the law).[13] This view lacks a proper understanding of the function of the law. As Kaiser (1978) puts it, "Far from being a legalistic code or a hypothetical means of earning one's salvation, the law was a means of maintaining fellowship with Yahweh [God] - not the grounds of establishing it" (p. 63). For our purposes, the razor's edge describes our goal in how we deliberate about ethical problems. When faced with an ethical issue, we can handle it too judgmentally or too loosely. We want to handle it just right so that the right amount of justice is meted out in a gracious way. It is this type of response that builds up the organization.

---

[13] This is the basis for a theme found in most American movies produced after 1970, that in order to have genuine life you have to *break the rules*. Sproul (1986) comments on this common attitude resulting from antinomianism: "There are times when a man has to push his principles aside and do the right thing" (p. 41). The assumption is that justice *gets in the way* of experiencing genuine life. This thinking is a somewhat correct reaction to legalism, but misses the mark by lacking an understanding of the correct narrow way (an accurate rendering of both justice and mercy) that Jesus teaches.

Sproul (1986) summarizes the different types of legalism and antinomianism based on historic Christian teaching. I will just comment on a few of his categories that are most pertinent to our discussions on analyzing business ethics problems.

One form of legalism is adding to the law. In making ethical decisions in organizations, this means that you evaluate a person's unethical behavior as more severe than your organizational standards dictate. (It is also possible that your organizational policies can become legalistic, but that has to do with how you set up your ethics program, something we will discuss in chapter 6.) Let me give you an example of this concept. I run a small consulting business and rent a box from an office service company to receive business-related mail. The company also receives my packages, which helps me because someone is always available to sign for UPS and other deliveries. On two occasions in a six-month period, the office service could not find my packages. On the second occasion, I had to ask at least three times for the package and finally had to take time from my schedule to call UPS to trace the package, only to find out that someone at the office service company had already signed for it, indicating that they had indeed received it weeks earlier. A few months later, my box renewal came up and I simply asked the owner if I could receive a credit on my yearly payment for these two inconveniences. The owner went ballistic and basically said that he no longer wanted my business because I brought up this matter.[14] I was able to calm him down and continue my business there. But this is an example of someone overreacting to an ethical issue. Is it right for him to give me a credit for the poor performance of his organization? I think so, but he disagreed. His basic response was "it was an honest mistake." That is certainly his prerogative based on his organizational ethical standards. But I think the balanced reaction is

---

[14] It is possible that the owner was manipulating me by using an attacking leadership style (see footnote comments on Darwin and leadership earlier in the book). Perhaps he just wanted to avoid refunding my money because it would lower his revenues. He wanted me to feel guilty for *upsetting* him so that I would acquiesce.

simply to refuse my request instead of choosing to dismiss a long-standing customer. Unfortunately this form of legalism occurs all too often in organizations. Ethical decisions are made based on personal preference instead of according to organizational standards. Thus personal (wild card) categories are added to the law. Adding to the law is perhaps the worst form of legalism because it can totally stifle an organization. It inhibits creativity and rewards those who keep the legalistic rules instead of those who further the purposes of the organization.[15]

Another form of legalism is majoring on the minors. Things that are less important are treated as if they are of utmost importance. This happens often in organizations where people focus their ethics on the bureaucratic policies instead of real ethical issues. My wife and I decided to enroll our then two year old daughter in a church mother's day out program in our community so that my wife would have time to study while pursuing her Masters degree in Biology. My wife visited a large main line church with a promising program that was close to our home. She was told that she had to pay an $85 registration fee and the tuition for the first and last month (of school year) of the program. Then she was told that she had to complete all of the paper work in order to be officially accepted into the program. After looking at the information more closely, we decided that this organization went out of their way to aggressively charge customers. You could say they were "competing effectively," but their policies seemed extreme to us for a church-based mother's day out program. Because of our concern about their financial policies, we decided not to use their services. Six days later, we went to

---

[15] I think most secularists caricature Christianity this way. They ignore the heart of the Gospel (truth **and grace**) and set up a straw man of Christianity (wrongly) based on legalism (particularly adding to the law) and then denounce it as stifling. In taking this stance, they fail to take into account the many verses in the New Testament by Jesus (not to mention the rest of the New Testament) that criticize this very legalism as demonstrated by the Scribes and Pharisees. Also, Secularists ignore the fact that Political Correctness is simply a different form of Legalism based on *wild card* personal standards. Thus personal preferences like *all smoking is evil* and *SUVs kill our environment* are placed (by some) at the same ethical level (at least rhetorically) as drug addiction and murder.

the director of the program and asked for a refund. We were told that they would not refund the $85 deposit because it was "nonrefundable." I countered with the point that we had not received any goods or services for that $85, ergo they were ripping us off. Also, we had not completed the application that theoretically was the basis for acceptance into the program. Then I was told that this policy was in place because they had to "hire teachers" and had to "enter our data." At bottom line, it was "in the brochure." I got the feeling that the director (who appeared to have strengths in administration) had been burned by customers in the past and her financial goal through her bureaucratic policies was that she was not going to be burned again. So the organization took our money without ever officially receiving us into the program. Is it right to charge people money and give them nothing in return? I don't think so. But, evidently this ethical standard is not as important to this organization as doing what's in the brochure. Ironically, their actions confirmed my concern about their restrictive financial policies. We ended up finding another program at a different church and ended up paying thousands of dollars to this church during the years both of my children attended. This type of legalism blinds people and keeps them from taking a step back and truly evaluating a situation from an ethical point of view. A gross example of this abuse can be seen by the workers who processed Jews for extermination during the Holocaust.[16] They worked hard (which is a good ethic), but to what end? They certainly majored on the minors.

A third type of legalism is found very often in business. It is called loopholism: "getting around the law by legal and moral technicalities" (Sproul, 1986, p. 38). In some ways, this is a form of antinomianism (because the goal is to not live up to the law), but still included here. The goal here is to appear to keep a rule while not being impacted by it. This technique was rampant in American corporate accounting practices in the 1990s and both business and government in the first

---

[16] See movie *Schindler's List* and scene where desks and office equipment is set up to process Jews for extermination camps.

part of the 21st century. Theoretically, accounting practices are used to show an accurate picture of a company's financial position. The meaning of *accurate* was stretched like a rubber band in the 1990s when accountants used techniques to show a positive picture for investment purposes regardless of the actual condition of the company.

Here we can refer to our earlier discussion of situation ethics as an example of loopholism. Sproul (1986) briefly describes it: "The general basis for situation ethics is that there is one and only one absolute, normative ethical principle to which every human being is bound - the law of love, a law which is not always easy to discern" (p. 41). The result of this norm is that sometimes you have to ignore your ethical principles to do the loving thing. Keep in mind two points about this norm. I think this point of view is a secular reaction to legalism (particularly majoring on the minors). This is OK in itself. Legalism is not good. However, the problem with this point of view is that another ethical layer is simply added above your normal ethical standards. The question still remains: what is the ethical basis for this new standard? Secondly, there is a denial that love can be found in normal ethical standards. In the Christian point of view, we can trust that the God of love knows what He is doing when He gives us His commands. To obey His commands is to live out love.[17]

Why this detailed discussion on the narrow way in this section on analyzing all of the information, looking at all sides? The reason is that you can gather helpful information and still come to the wrong conclusions if you err in applying your ethical standard to the side of legalism or antinomianism. You want to judge fairly based on the standards of your organization, nothing more or nothing less. You

---

[17] See 1 John 5:2, "By this we know that we love the children of God, when we love God and keep His commandments." Note that our love for others is directly tied to our love for God, which is tied to obedience to what He commands. The Christian life is based on trust that God knows what He is talking about and we don't. The situation ethicists are not willing to trust God's directives but want to be able to trump them with their own understanding of *love*.

must judge fairly and not be affected by the type of people you are dealing with.[18]

Make a decision based on your organizational standards and what is good for all

Make a decision based on your organizational ethical standards while taking into consideration what is good for all the people in your organization and as much as possible to the individuals concerned. It is critical here that you understand your organizational standards (as stated previously) and make your decision based on those standards. Keep in mind that leaders who are acting unethically merit rougher punishment because of their influence on others.[19]

Implement the decision ethically

Now that you understand what actions to take, implement the decision ethically. A number of years ago, a friend who led a private school since its inception (almost 20 years) was summarily dismissed by the board for various reasons. The reasons given for dismissal were questionable, but the way the board implemented the decision was more disturbing. My friend was locked out of the building without warning and ushered off the premises. This was no way to treat someone who had done so much for that institution. I am sure the board gave much thought about

---

[18] See Galatians 3:28, "There is neither Jew nor Greek, there is neither slave nor free, there is neither male nor female; for you are all one in Christ Jesus." The point is that we are all the same when we stand before the standards of Jesus Christ. We are all accountable in the same way and (conversely) should all receive the same consideration of mercy as appropriate. See also James 2:1-9 where partiality is specifically called a *sin*.

[19] See Matthew 18:6, "But whoever causes one of these little ones who believe in Me to sin, it would be better for him if a millstone were hung around his neck, and he were drowned in the depth of the sea." See also James 3:1, "My brethren, let not many of you become teachers, knowing that we shall receive a stricter judgment." The point here is that leaders are more accountable because of their influence on others.

how to handle this situation (remove my friend) but gave no regard or thought on how to implement the solution. And this issue did not appear in any way to involve an ethical issue!

The Scripture gives guidance, "If possible, so far as it depends on you, live peaceably with all." (Romans 12:18, ESV). Organizations should do all they can to deal with a bad person who is involved with unethical activity with peace but it may not be possible.[20]

Discuss the lessons learned

Finally, learn from the situation so that you can avoid this problem in the future. You want to learn from the situation without punishing everyone within the organization through excessive rules and regulations. You want to be wise so that you can prevent the problem from occurring again. If you do not learn from the problem, it is likely to occur again. You want to be wise and avoid foolishness by taking proactive steps in order to ensure that the problem does not occur once again.[21]

WHAT IS AN ETHICAL ISSUE?

In the movie *Up Close and Personal*, Robert Redford and Michelle Pfeiffer play television news reporters. Redford is the experienced broadcaster and he is helping Pfeiffer find her way. The movie provides an interesting commentary on the news and the ethical issues related to reporting. Perhaps the defining moment of the movie is when Pfeiffer (after heeding Redford's advice) receives an award for her professional reporting. She takes an ethical tone as she talks about her success to a rapt audience. She exhorts them to tell the story. This appears to be the

---

[20] See 2 Timothy 3:1-8, "But understand this, that in the last days there will come times of difficulty. ... [people] always learning but never able to arrive at a knowledge of the truth. Avoid such people... men corrupted in mind ..." (ESV) (brackets added).

[21] See Proverbs 26:11, "As a dog returns to his own vomit, So a fool repeats his folly."

essence of "ethical" journalism according to the film, to fully tell the story. However, I beg to differ. Telling the story is indeed important. But, the bigger and more important issue is: which story do you tell? In the news, like business ethics, there are many topics to talk about. Why are some deemed important and others are ignored? My point is that your business ethics foundation will determine which issues are ethically important and others not. Obviously, companies need to uphold the law. But, beyond that there are other ethical issues to consider.

Some would say that after keeping the law, the only ethic is to make money for stockholders. This is fine, but is this not the love of money problem that we addressed in chapter 3? The point of the Christian view is that going after money as the first priority creates problems.[22] The conundrum of the Christian ethic in business is that you will make more money in the long run if you do not seek it as your first priority. Also, what about entrepreneurs? If making money for stockholders is the ultimate ethic, what about companies that do not have stockholders? Is it all about making money for the owner? Then you begin asking the question, how much money? When is enough, enough?[23]

Each type of business will face different ethical problems. You must think about the three to five (or more) ethical problems that your people will face in your type of business. Tell your people about these problems and the behavioral chain that leads people to act unethically.

---

[22] See Cavanagh's (1998, pp. 182-183) comments about Schumpeter's view of capitalism. He predicts the demise of capitalism because of the results that occur when capitalism is successful: "As free enterprise is successful, human needs are satisfied and opportunities for investment are fewer. That same success undermines the need for, and so the position and prestige of the entrepreneur, who is no longer dominant or even highly respected in society" (Cavanagh, 1998, pp. 182-183).

[23] See Gehrman (2003), "Is the question 'What's your number?' aimed at finding how much money we need, or is it how much we want; because if it is how much we want, the desire will probably never be satisfied. ... The true believers, in the power of money to make them happy, can lead them and their organizations down a path of destruction not dreams."

Then, teach them exactly what you want them to do based on the company's ethical standards and guidelines so that each employee is familiar with these standards and guidelines. This is one of the most effective components of a great business ethics program.[24]

As mentioned previously, to solve an ethical issue, you must be aware that an ethics violation is taking place. It is critical that you become experts in your business so that you can determine when something unusual (unethical) takes place. Your ethical point of view will determine what an ethical issue is.

Now, let us look at two ethical issues and how we might look at them from the Christian point of view. The first issue is not addressed in most business ethics books, but it needs to be addressed as a Christian issue. The second issue is raised as an issue by secular ethicists. We will examine both issues from our Christian framework.

Human Nature

From the Christian view, three important facts emerge about the people with whom we do business. First, people are basically sinful and they do not by nature desire to follow God's principles.[25] Secondly, people are not as bad as they could be because of God's common concern for the world, so they may obey God's principles in spite of themselves. Thirdly, people are valuable and worthy of respect and fair treatment because all people are created in God's image and are objects of His concern.

---

[24] See Ephesians 4:17-24 where Paul tells Christians to stop using the old, sinful patterns of behavior. In your business, encourage your people to stop carrying out business in the old, unethical way. Then Paul says to change your thinking and put on the new ways. He goes on in Ephesians 4 to give specific details of what he means. This is what you must do for your people, give specific examples of what you want them to do in difficult ethical situations.

[25] See Romans 3, especially 22b-23, "For there is no difference; for all have sinned and fall short of the glory of God ..." This verse (and the rest of chapter 3) argues that we all have a common condition; we are **not** diverse at the center of our natures. We **all** fall short of God's standards.

We reflect our love for God by how well we treat others, Christian or non-Christian.[26]

Let's look at the ethical issue of human nature and how you need to take it into consideration when carrying out business. Chewning, Eby, and Roels (1990) talk about the ramifications of our first principle, that people are sinful by nature, and how that impacts solving (and preventing) ethical problems; "Prior knowledge of possible temptations and an effective plan to eliminate the temptation are the two best defenses against immoral behavior. ... We must take sin seriously in the business environment and find ways to use both positive and negative rewards to help people control their behavior" (p. 42). How do you react to people who are trying to do you harm? Our natural reaction is to become defensive and combative. Romans 12:21 gives a different approach: "Do not be overcome by evil, but overcome evil with good."[27] Don't sacrifice your standards merely because others treat you poorly. Do not let others control you. That certainly does not mean that you have to compromise with those who wish you evil. Having confidence in your own views allows you to argue strongly for a common ground for doing business that you can live with.

---

[26] See 1 John 2:9-10, "He who says he is in the light, and hates his brother, is in darkness until now. He who loves his brother abides in the light, and there is no cause for stumbling in him." See also 1 John 3:10-11, "In this the children of God and the children of the devil are manifest: Whoever does not practice righteousness is not of God, nor is he who does not love his brother. For this is the message that you heard from the beginning, that we should love one another."

[27] This is not a passive posture. Acquiescing to the evil person's wishes while continuing to be *nice* to them is not what this the Scripture has in mind. Doing good to a person who does evil to you puts pressure on him to do the right thing. If he then does evil to you again, he is doubly guilty. See Proverbs 17:13, "Whoever rewards evil for good, Evil will not depart from his house." Doing good to a person is a very active posture. You are aggressively expecting him to do the right thing in return. Keep in mind that your ability to do good may be limited with an enemy. Romans 12:18 says, "If it is possible, as much as depends on you, live peaceably with all men." See also Matthew 5:40 where Jesus says, "But I say unto you, love your enemies, bless those who curse you, do good to those who hate you ..."

Our second principle regarding human nature is that people are not as bad as they could be because of God's common concern for the world so they may outwardly obey God's principles in spite of themselves. The important application of this point is that as Christians we can often find a common ground for doing business. God's principles are useful even though a person is not a Christian. So, for business reasons some may apply a reflection of Christian principles even though they do not believe. Even though their motives are not consistent, we can still do business with them.

Most business leaders do not have the proper perspective when facing the human nature of their employees and other stakeholders. Either there is no accountability (antinomianism) or leaders overreact and set up excessive bureaucracy (legalism). Friedman (1962) highlights this tension using a different institution for his example but it still applies, "Our minds tell us, and history confirms, that the great threat to freedom is the concentration of power. Government is necessary to preserve our freedom, it is an instrument through which we can exercise our freedom; yet by concentrating power in political hands, it is also a threat to freedom" (p. 2). Chewning, Eby, and Roels (1990) describe a healthy leadership attitude when facing the problem of maintaining ethics in your organization (which we have discussed earlier in the book),

> Three forces form a moral magnetic field and help keep us on a positive course of behavior: love or commitment to internal moral standards; positive reward for good behavior; and negative consequences for inappropriate behavior. If any one of the three ceases to function, enormous pressure is placed on the others.[28] (p. 43)

---

[28] This is one of the problems with regulation. Regulations are put in place to enforce rules and standards, the assumption being that they are de facto ethical. But, those who regulate can also act unethically. Another problem with regulation is that it normally punishes the people who are trying to act ethically (forces them to do additional work in order to show *compliance*). Unethical people will simply ignore

Diversity

Let's look at the issue of diversity as our next example. Diversity is seen as an important ethical issue by a number of companies (for example Booz Allen & Hamilton included it as one of its core values when I worked there). Companies often mean by this concept that they should not discriminate, that they should respect differences between groups, and that they should do all they can to allow groups to celebrate their distinctives. This can lead to affirmative action in hiring, setting up different ethnic organizations within the company, and diversity training where employees are encouraged to become knowledgeable about different "cultural characteristics."

Diversity is helpful to organizations but is it really an ethical issue in itself? If it is, what is its nature? Let's look at what the scriptures say about this topic. Paul emphasizes our unity as individuals, "For you are all sons of God through faith in Christ Jesus. … There is neither Jew nor Greek, there is neither slave nor free, there is neither male nor female; for you are all one in Christ Jesus." (Galatians 3:26, 28) Some in the church were trying to say that certain people could not fully become Christians until they performed "extra" ceremonies.[29] Paul argued strongly that it is only by faith that anyone comes to Christ. And there is NO distinction among those who come. So, Paul argues that

---

the regulation or immediately look for a way around it (*loopholism*). So, all that we are doing is complicating the original ethical problem. I think the solution is actively enforcing the law. Adding regulations does not make people comply. Enforcing good laws does.

[29] One of the additional ceremonies that these *Judaizers* required was circumcision for males. Paul argued strongly that this was not needed for salvation. In fact he grew quite angry at those who would add to the law in this way. See Galatians 5:6, 12-13a, "For in Christ Jesus neither circumcision nor uncircumcision avails anything, but faith working through love. … I would wish that those who trouble you would even cut themselves off! For you, brethren, have been called to liberty." This is a classic example of the effective use of sarcasm. Paul is basically saying, "You think circumcision will help you towards salvation? Then don't mess around. Go all the way. Cut the whole thing off. That should really make you righteous!"

we should not discriminate because of race ("Jew nor Greek"), position ("slave nor free"), or sex ("male nor female"). I think we all agree that this is an important plank in the understanding of "diversity." But notice the unity that he suggests: "you are all one." So somehow in the Christian understanding of diversity in organizations, there must be a unifying theme. For business, that unifying theme is the ethical statement for the organization. Let's explore this notion further.

Paul talks about organizations in Romans 12. The organization is the church but the principles apply to any organization, including business. He says in Romans 12:3-5:

> For I say, through the grace given to me, to everyone who is among you, not to think of himself more highly than he ought to think, but to think soberly, as God has dealt to each one a measure of faith. For as we have many members in one body, but all the members do not have the same function, so we, being many, are one body in Christ, and individually members of one another.

The verse goes on to discuss the fact that each person has received different gifts to use. This verse confirms the first aspect of diversity. There is a unity in the midst of the differences ("one body"). However there is also diversity ("all the members do not have the same function"). But the distinctiveness of the Christian position, which has ramifications for our understanding of diversity as a business ethics issue, is the diversity that Romans talks about is based on our INDIVIDUAL diversity not our GROUP diversity. This important principle becomes apparent in the phrase from Romans 12:5: "... so we, *being many* [we are diverse], are *one body in Christ* [we have unity amidst the diversity], and *individually* [people are seen as individuals in their diversity, not as members of a particular group] members of one another ..." (emphasis added) (brackets added). To focus on groups as your point of diversity robs individuals of their opportunity to be unique and engenders looking at individuals according to group stereotypes (which is the very thing diversity is supposedly trying to do away with). Wood (2003) illustrates this problem as it applies to university settings: "it [wrong view of diversity] validates and reinforces the dehumanizing habit of judging people by stereotypes. ... Black students, for example, are routinely called on to present 'black' points of view and are criticized if their views do not fit what their teachers consider appropriate to the students' 'social position'" (pp. 135-136). (brackets added)

Should we therefore ban special interest groups from meeting in business? No, I don't think so. But I think the groups should be formed because of interest, not because of racial, positional (managers vs. regular employees), or sexual categories. I think this works against a healthy notion of diversity.[30] There is an important unity among people and the diversity comes from our uniqueness as individuals, not our belonging primarily to a particular group. I think this is the Biblical model.

Your action item for this chapter is to create your own "steps for solving ethical problems." You need an action plan to use when you face ethical problems in your organization to make sure that you handle the problem thoroughly and professionally. But, it perhaps more important to prevent problems in the first place. That is the subject of our next chapter!

---

[30] It is interesting to consider Wood's explanation regarding the roots of the modern "diversity" movement. Wood (2003) states, "For at least a century before Darwin published *The Origin of Species* and for half a century after, the dominant theory linking human biological diversity and cultural diversity was the theory of race. Racialist theories are attempts to account for human diversity as though that diversity were *primarily* a matter of distinct biological varieties. Through Darwin and his many successors, we have learned to see natural diversity as a tremendously positive aspect of our world" (p. 86). See also his continued arguments on pages 86-87 of his book where he says that this notion of "diversity" encourages racial profiling instead of accepting people for who they are on the inside. "Diversity" may be important to some as a political issue as a way of furthering conflict among classes.

CHAPTER 5 QUESTIONS FOR REVIEW

1. What are the two major applications of business ethics?

2. Explain why it is important to know your organizational standards as well as the business operations when you are trying to apply ethics in your organization.

3. What approach does Scripture recommend for solving inter-personal problems?

4. List and comment briefly on the book's suggested approach for solving ethical problems.

5. Why is Step 1 so critical in the process of solving ethical problems?

6. What are the two roles to keep in mind when gathering information (Step 3)?

7. Explain the razor's edge and why it is important for Step 4. Discuss legalism and antinomianism and how they impact the razor's edge.

8. Come up with our own "steps for solving ethical problems" that you can use in your current or future organization.

9. How do we determine what is an ethical issue?

10. What are potential ethical challenges in the industry in which you work? Describe a possible situation and how your firm (or a future one you might join) deals with the potential of such a threat through policies and practices (for instance, employee handbook, training, progressive discipline, rewards, etc.). How might you change it?

MAKE ETHICS WORK BY SETTING UP AN ETHICS PROGRAM

THE GOAL OF AN EFFECTIVE ethics program is to reap the benefits of having an ethical culture (see chapter 1 of book on "Why ethics are good for business"). Building an ethical culture can help an organization gain a sustainable competitive advantage in the marketplace.[1] So, there are financial considerations as well as ethical ones (it's the right thing to do) in setting up an effective ethics (also called "ethics and compliance") program.

There are two basics components to address when setting up an effective ethics program. You must comply with the law (called ethical compliance). This is a legal function best suited for the organization's lawyers. You must make sure that your organization keeps all of the appropriate laws. This involves providing proper information and training for all personnel regarding pertinent laws and documenting those activities. Risk management is an aspect of this work, realizing that the costs and bad publicity associated with ethical violations are not worth the cost of proper compliance training and oversight. There are also investigative functions to carry out when it appears that the law has been broken (see previous chapter). This function is more preventative.

---

[1] However, keep in mind that this is a long-term perspective and companies may not care about long-term success but only what can be done immediately. We have argued (see section on "Five Main Principles") that a long-term focus reflects Scripture.

You want to stay out of trouble. It deals with external values, those that are imposed from without (by government). Even though we do not cover this topic in detail, it does not mean that the topic is unimportant.

The second component of an effective ethics program is proactive. You want to develop the ethical acumen of your people based on the ethics of your organization. You want people to not only keep the law (you might say the bare minimum) but you want them to do more. You want your people to actively live out the ethics of your organization (we might call values-based compliance) in their day to day business lives. It is at this point that a company becomes truly ethical. You develop this aspect of the program by having great key leaders who actively model the company standards, to the point of having ethics influence strategic planning. As Chappell (1993) puts it "beliefs drive strategy" (p. x). This calls for transformational leadership at all levels where the transformation takes place through modeling and influence and proper punishment when necessary, not through coercion.[2] As you can see in the graphic below, the law and what is ethical may overlap, but doing the right thing often means doing more than the bare minimum of the law.

---

[2] For an example see De Pree's (1989) description of leadership, "In many organizations there are two kinds of leaders - both hierarchical and roving leaders. In special situations, the hierarchical leader is obliged to identify the roving leader, then to support and follow him or her, and also to exhibit the grace that enables the roving leader to lead. It's not easy to let someone else take the lead. To do this demands a special openness and the ability to recognize what is best for the organization and how best to respond to an issue" (p. 42). Sharing power without giving up responsibility is an important trait of transformational leadership. De Pree's *roving* leadership is one example of this trait.

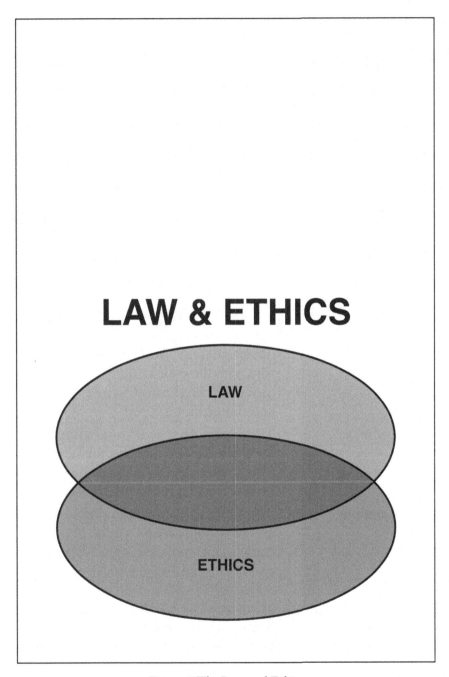

Figure 8 The Law and Ethics

Let's start with the organizational structure. Where should the ethics office appear on the organization chart? First of all, the CEO of the company needs to own the ethics program. He or she needs to realize that example is the most powerful communicator of an ethics program. The ethics officer is the leader put in charge of implementing the CEO's program. The goal is to improve business for everyone. The ethics office usually appears in the following locations: Legal department, Personnel office, and the Diversity office (often part of Human Resource). I disagree with these organizational locations. I think the ethics office should report directly to the CEO. However, I also think that the ethics office should carry out most of the work in a matrix relationship with other components of the company. Here is an example of those relationships:

Department	Collaboration with Ethics
Legal	On compliance issues, legal department may well play the lead role with the ethics office providing administration and communication support
Personnel	The ethics office will work with the Personnel department for hiring and orientation issues (so proper ethics training takes place).
Operations	The ethics office will provide advice for operations, develop training materials for ethical issues and how to resolve them. Also, the ethics office will consult operations for expertise on determining when ethical violations are taking place.

Figure 9 Departmental Contributions to Business Ethics Function

The importance of the proper position in the organization cannot be overemphasized. As some have said, a good person will lose to a bad organization and processes every time.[3]

I endorse this organizational position for the ethics function for a couple of reasons. A few years ago, I spoke with an ethics leader in a large corporation. The company had recently moved their ethics office to a different department that was less visible to the organization. This action alone communicated the diminishing importance that the organization placed on their ethics program. Keep in mind that small businesses are not large enough to hire a separate ethics officer. However, you can still note the ethics function in its proper place on your organizational chart even though someone who also has a different role carries it out.

You have set up your ethics function. You realize the importance of compliance and have received legal counsel in making sure you are keeping the law. Now you want to go further. You want to prevent ethical issues from coming up and you want to actively promote goodness as a company. This is where you deal with (again from a theological perspective) the sins of omission; where you don't do the things that you should be doing. You want to prevent ethical problems and promote goodness by setting up an active and vibrant ethics program. Chewning, Eby, and Roels (1990) concur: "It is very important to plan. ... Many ethical disasters can be avoided if we shape formal ethics policies and educate our employees about ethical responses before the actual situation confronts them" (p. 242).

You set up your ethics program by addressing four key areas:

- Recruitment
- Orientation (socialization)
- On going discussions with employees, particularly in regard to new ethical issues that emerge. These are best handled through

---

[3] See Rummler & Brache (1995), "If you pit a good performer against a bad system, the system will win almost every time. We spend too much time 'fixing' people who are not broken, and not enough time fixing organization systems that are broken" (pp. 13-14). An entire book could be written on how business ethics relates to Rummler-Brache's organizational (operational) improvement approach.

scenarios where common issues are presented and then what should be done in those situations.

- Development of Key Leaders (Ethics certification program) which includes imbedding ethics in the strategic planning of the company.

Let's look at each one in more detail.

RECRUITMENT

Take pains to find people that are a good ethical match for your organization. Ask them to tell you their personal view of business ethics and how that influences their work. Give them ethics scenarios that are pertinent to your type of business and ask them what they would do. Have them tell you **why** they give the answers they give on the scenarios, which reveals their worldview. Also watch their behavior as they are going through recruitment exercises. For example, Southwest Airlines (at least at one point) had potential recruits give presentations. But the real evaluation was how they listened to the presentations of others. This showed teamwork and concern for other people.

Background checks are important. If you do discover questionable information, confront your potential employee with it, watch their reaction, and give them the chance to explain. There are two sides to every story. You want to be wise about the type of people you will hire. Follow up on all references and confirm degrees, previous employment and accomplishments.

ORIENTATION

When setting up your orientation program, you want to keep in mind that this is a main part of your overall effort towards socialization. Socialization is the process of identifying "who we are" (based on company ethics statement) and then encouraging members of the organization to act accordingly. As Cavanagh (1998) points out, there are two basic kinds of socialization: formal and informal: "Formal socialization is the planned and deliberate attempt by the organization to affect the attitudes of members. Informal socialization takes place among members through ordinary interaction" (p. 198). Formal socialization includes classes, evaluation, organizational documents, and what is spoken in public forums. Informal socialization includes what people (particularly leaders) actually do in specific situations, what people are rewarded and punished for, what people say at informal company activities and during informal conversations.

Socialization is a two-edged sword. You can increase moral, build ethics, and improve productivity by gaining uniformity between formal and informal socialization. However if they differ, you at best spend time and money on formal programs and activities that are trumped and contradicted by actual events. At worst, this discrepancy can cause big problems in the organization. Because, it can be said that informal socialization is more powerful than formal. I worked with Enron (ECT Computer Training group) as an on-site contractor between 1993 and 1998. About halfway through my four and a half years, Enron hired a new VP of Information Systems. We had a large meeting at a fancy hotel during the day to discuss future strategy. At night we continued our activities at a popular local bar. After about an hour of food and drinks and talking, the new VP and his leadership team arrived. One of the first events after his arrival was "the scantily clad young lady pouring shots into open mouths." And guess who was the first person to participate? Yes, amidst shouts and cheers, the new VP was the first one. Then one by one, his leadership team performed the same ritual. Now, don't get me wrong I am not condemning these individuals for going through "the scantily clad young lady pouring shots into open mouths" routine. It was a bar and this is a free country. I was simply struck by what they were communicating regarding socialization. Socialization could have been more powerful if the new VP had taken time to walk around to actually meet and personally welcome each individual who attended.

Orientation is the critical time in the life of a new employee to influence them towards the company's standards. Therefore, I recommend that the CEO begin the orientation with a welcome and statement about the company ethical standards along with the vision for the organization. Along with the CEO's words, you should communicate the benefits of being ethical (see chapter 1 of this book). Let people know your standards, rewards for embracing the standards, and consequences for ignoring the standards. Give scenarios of common ethical issues that your employees face. Show the common (wrong) way that people might respond to tempting situations. Then show them how you want them to respond. This is a powerful endorsement of the practical use of your standards. You also need to make new employees aware of legal and regulatory compliance issues. However, you should make a distinction between these compliance-based issues and other ethical issues. Take time to present how ethics are a proactive part of your organization. If community service is part of your ethics program, allow them to participate in a service activity as part of their orientation.

ON GOING

The company must develop an excellent ethics statement. It does not have to be large, but it does need to accurately reflect the worldview of the key leaders of the organization. It also must truly reflect the organization so that actions will remain consistent with the ethics statement.

Make ethics part of the evaluation process. People must be promoted and otherwise awarded by excellent performance DONE ETHICALLY. Departmental meetings are an important way to identify particular ethical issues that impact the department and how they should be handled. There are a number of other means for continuing to build ethics in your organization through effective promotion:

- Flyers
- Posters

- Small cards with ethics statement (including ID badges)
- E-mails
- Special meetings

You must also set up a means for employees to report ethical violations. This function must remain confidential and protect the reporting employee. However, the accused individual must receive a fair investigation, and if necessary be confronted by their accuser. It is important to put together a solid investigation team who is well schooled in the methods of resolving ethical problems (as mentioned earlier in this book).

LEADERSHIP DEVELOPMENT

It is important to include business ethics as part of the leadership development process. Retreats are a good way to develop ethics in senior leadership, particularly as it relates to strategic planning. Encourage ethics certification as part of the training for advancement. Imbed ethics in a proactive way in business strategy.

Emphasize with leaders an approach to effectively implement company business ethics. The importance in setting up company ethics is not just to increase regulation but to actually enforce the standards that are in place. This is accomplished by taking the following approach, taken from Genesis 2.[4]

1. Tell each person what they can do
2. Tell each person what they cannot do
3. Tell them the consequences of doing what they cannot do
4. Enforce

---

[4] Genesis 2:16-17 says, "And the LORD God commanded the man saying, 'Of every tree of the garden you may freely eat [#1 - what they **can** do]; but of the tree of the knowledge of good and evil you shall not eat [#2 - what they **cannot** do], for in the day that you eat of it you shall surely die [#3 - **consequences**]." (brackets added)

CHAPTER 6 QUESTIONS FOR REVIEW

1. What is the main business reason for setting up an ethics program?

2. What are the two basic components of an ethics program?

3. What is a "key" starting point to proactively getting ethics into your organization?

4. Discuss where the ethics function should appear in the organizational structure and why.

5. What are the four key areas to address through your ethics program?

6. Explain "socialization" and its role in the Orientation part of the ethics program.

7. List several ways to communicate ethics during the On-going part of the ethics program.

8. What basic guidelines does Genesis 2 give to leaders for setting up and running (at least part of) an effective ethics program?

9. Describe your own organization's corporate culture (and role of business ethics) and discuss the role of leadership in development of the culture. Would you alter their approach in any way if you were building the ethical culture?

10. Write your own plan for setting up an ethics program in your current (or future) organization.

MAKE ETHICS WORK OUTSIDE YOUR ORGANIZATION

TO THIS POINT IN THE book, we have focused on ethics within the organization and towards primary stakeholders (those to whom the organization owes a fiduciary, or financial/legal, responsibility). Now we will shift our focus to ethics outside the organization and to, we might say, secondary stakeholders. Specifically, what is an organization's responsibility to the community and, we could add, the environment; called *corporate social responsibility* (CSR)? As a key leader in your organization, you need to prioritize on building the ethical culture of your organization, but you also want to think about applying your ethical principles to those external to the organization as well. It is beyond the scope of this book to cover this topic of CSR in detail. However, it is important to lay down some basic principles that can help organizations think through this sticky subject; which means asking the right questions and developing a plan that works for your organization and the community.

THE ISSUE

In public discourse, it is important to not use a slogan (or slogans) to "explain" a complex issue.[1] Perhaps nowhere is this insight more

---

[1] For example, saying that the housing bubble problem (early part of 21st century) was "caused" by "greedy mortgage companies" is missing the mark. In reality,

pertinent than in the area of CSR. Slogans play a role when helping people remember truthful and helpful information. But slogans, in the public arena, are often used to evoke emotional responses and to manipulate. Reasoned argumentation is the Biblical verbal vehicle for persuasion,[2] and should be our method as well.

Let's start by clarifying the meaning of the term *corporate social responsibility*. The immediate question is: "responsible to who"? or to "what"? Also, the term "social" seems vague, because no particular person or group seems to be mentioned as making up "society," which must mean that everyone is included; which means corporations have a responsibility to "everyone" which is untenable. So, what is the scope of that "responsibility" and what standard determines the scope? So, for example, can any person or group who shouts loudly claim to "speak" for "everyone" and thus set the "standard" which others (i.e. companies) may unwittingly accept? The word "corporate" could be mistaken to imply that "responsibility" for others outside the organization only applies to large companies (corporations), and the expected word meaning ("corporate" = "communal") is, again, unclear. Others agree that the definition of CSR is vague, leading some to say "there are as many definitions of CSR as there are writers" (Amaeshiand & Adin, 2007, p. 4);[3] thus illustrating that worldview shapes an understanding

---

the issue resulted from a variety of circumstances and entities and individuals, including the Federal government and also, yes, "greedy mortgage companies" and individuals (for an excellent overview of the housing bubble problem, see Thomas Sowell's book: *The Housing Boom and Bust*). This example relates to our topic because we could ague that part of the problem was the stated "desire" to provide "affordable housing" (another slogan). Obviously, there is nothing wrong with trying to remove barriers to allow individuals to obtain housing, but a slogan to "provide affordable housing" is vague and can mask other agendas.

[2] See Paul; "Therefore, knowing the fear of the Lord, we persuade others." (2 Corinthians 5:11, ESV) This is true even when the other party is verbally attacking: "... When reviled, we bless; when persecuted, we endure, *when slandered, we entreat.*" (1 Corinthians 4:12) (emphasis added)

[3] See Ruddell's (2014) article (*Corporate Social Responsibility: Helping Students Understand The Historical And Modern Construct For Future Results*) on the subject for more detail.

of CSR. If that is the case, what might be a more accurate meaning of CSR?

From a Christian worldview, we could say the CSR stands for "covenantal social responsibility"; which here focuses on ethical obligations to people outside of the organization. Christians have a responsibility to God and others that they know and/or people God brings across their paths.[4] It is certainly within the Covenantal notion to commit to doing good to all those impacted by the organization, particularly the poor and defenseless. The Covenantal model suggests that we have a commitment to look after "... not only our own interests, but also the interests of others" (Philippians 2:1-4, ESV) and we find out about the interests of others by getting to know them.[5]

If CSR entails helping people (particularly the poor), then how do we describe "poverty" and what does it mean to "help"? The Chalmers Center (Fikkert, n.d.) defines "poverty" this way:

> Poverty isn't just a lack of material things – it's rooted in broken relationships with God, self, others, and the rest of creation. We were created to glorify God, reflect His image, love one another, and steward the rest of creation. But the fall and sin marred what God originally created. As a result, none of us are experiencing the fullness of what God intended for us.

This explanation, based on a Christian worldview, means that none of us are better than anyone else, so there is no room for "paternalism"

---

4   Matthew 28:19 could be said to read "as you are going, make disciples ..." So, we need to help those who God brings across our paths, especially "the least of these" (see Matthew 25:40).

5   See Philippians 1:9, "And it is my prayer that your love may abound more and more, with knowledge and all discernment." (ESV) Love needs to hit home based on what the individual actually wants/needs, not whatever we feel like giving them. This is particularly pertinent when it comes to CSR and what it means to "help." And we can't find out what people want/need unless we develop a relationship with them and listen to them; "... let every person, be quick to hear, slow to speak ..." (James 1:19, ESV).

(notion that we know what is best for someone else without talking with and listening to them and finding out what they think is best for themselves). Also, work is fundamental to who we are as human beings based on creation (our part in "stewarding" God's Creation).[6] Finally, the key to "helping" those around us is to help restore relationships so that people can "bear their own load" (Galatians 6:5).

So, what are the ramifications for us as individuals and as business leaders? More needs to be said to explain and clarify. So, let's look at specific key principles (from Scripture) that give guidance, especially in helping the poor around us. Then we will discuss "program points" that will help organizations run the CSR functions as an extension of their business ethics program.

FIVE KEY CSR PRINCIPLES

Principle #1: Help the Poor

The Bible makes it clear that we are to help the poor and to uphold justice because that is part of the reason Christ came. In Luke 4:18-19, Jesus quotes Isaiah[7] and confirms that He and His work are the fulfillment of this prophesy,[8]

> "The Spirit of the Lord is upon me, because he has anointed
> me to proclaim good news to the poor, He has sent me to

---

[6] So, to not encourage work for those who are being helped (and who are able to work) is demeaning. See 2 Thessalonians 3:10-12, especially v10a; "... If anyone is not willing to work, let him not eat." (ESV) Also, see 1 Timothy 5:8 (which is directed to men): "But if anyone does not provide for his relatives, and especially for members of his household, he has denied the faith and is worse than an unbeliever." (ESV)

[7] See Luke 11:17, "And the scroll of the prophet Isaiah was given to him. ..." (ESV)

[8] See Luke 11:2-21, "And he rolled the scroll and gave it back to the attendant and sat down ... And he began to say to them, 'Today this Scripture has been fulfilled in your hearing.'" (ESV)

proclaim liberty to the captives and recovering of sight to the blind, to set at liberty those who are oppressed, to proclaim the year of the Lord's favor." (ESV)

So, individuals and organizations should do nothing to "oppress" poor and defenseless people and should do all they can to encourage self-sufficiency (freedom) of the poor and respect towards the poor and those with physical problems (i.e. "the blind"). But the "good news" is the same "good news" that goes out to all people; that Jesus Christ offers eternal life and hope for all.[9] Just as Jesus' offer and help go out to the poor, individuals and organizations should also do what they can to help.[10]

Amos 2:6-7 lists some of Israel's transgressions as an indictment and an explanation for why they are being punished: "... because they sell the righteous for silver, and the needy for a pair of sandals – those who trample the head of the poor into the dust of the earth and turn aside the way of the afflicted; ..." (ESV). Isaiah 58:6 echoes Amos' call for freedom, "'Is not this the fast that I choose: to loose the bonds of wickedness, to undo the straps of the yoke, to let the oppressed go free, and to break every yoke?'" (ESV) The Scripture also suggests that there is "benefit" for giving freely to those who can't really do anything for you: "And if you do good to those who do good to you, what benefit is that to you?" (Luke 6:33, NSV) 1 John 3:17 reminds us, "But if anyone has the world's goods and sees his brother in need, yet closes his heart against him, how does Gods love abide in him? Little children, let us not love in word or talk but in deed and in truth." (ESV) Showing love[11] includes helping someone you know when they need help which, again, means having a relationship with that person so you are personally

---

[9] "There is neither Jew nor Greek, *there is neither slave nor free* ... your are all one in Christ Jesus." (Galatians 3:28, ESV) (emphasis added)

[10] See below where we discuss what it really means to "help."

[11] See context in 1 John 3:16; "By this we know love ..." and fact that we don't really "know" love unless we do it.

aware of their need. So individuals in organizations should be free to help colleagues who face an economic or personal challenge.

But we should also help "strangers" when the opportunity presents itself. Isaiah 58:7 enjoins, "Is it not[12] to share your bread with the hungry and bring the homeless poor into your house; when you seek the naked, to cover him, and not to hide yourself from your own flesh?" (ESV) See also the story of the Good Samaritan (Luke 10:25-37) who was praised for helping a hurt man as he "journeyed." This parable is helpful because it answers the question "who is my neighbor"? And the answer is, your neighbor is someone who appears in front of you who has a legitimate need.[13] The obligation for those who are watching out for people in the community and others that you might impact while doing business is not really to go to a paternalistic "concern for the masses" sentiment only. The idea is that if you face a situation, you just do the right thing; "If you meet your enemy's ox or his donkey going astray, you shall bring it back to him ..." (Exodus 23:4-5, ESV). The New Testament talks about giving a cup of water (Matthew 10:42) which means meeting an immediate need of someone you come across.[14]

In summary, 2 Corinthians 9:6-7 reads, "The point is this: whoever sows sparingly will also reap sparingly, and whoever sows bountifully will also reap bountifully. Each one must give as he has decided in his heart, not reluctantly or under compulsion, for God loves a cheerful

---

[12] The purpose of real religion is to actually help those in front of you, not just "fast" physically. God is asking a rhetorical question through His prophet Isaiah about what "fasting" should really mean; which is to focus more on the Lord which should lead to providing help to others in real ways vs. simply participating in physical fasting for symbolic reasons.

[13] This goes back to our earlier discussion about the term *corporate social responsibility* and the problem of asking businesses to take care of "society," a vague reference to "masses," when the Bible seems to highlight looking out for opportunities to help in communities with people you actually come in contact with.

[14] See also Proverbs 3:27-29, "Do not withhold good from those to whom it is due, when it is in your power to do it. Do not say to your neighbor, 'Go and come again, tomorrow I will give it' – when you have it with you. Do not plan evil against your neighbor, who dwells trustingly beside you." (ESV)

giver." (ESV) Here, Paul stresses generosity and the fact that generosity yields "bountiful" benefits. Also, giving should be done freely, without coercion.[15]

Principle #2: Be Fair

James 2:1-17 asserts a focus on fairness; "My brothers, show no partiality as you hold the faith in our Lord Jesus Christ, the Lord of glory." (James 2:1, NSV) Show no favoritism (giving preference for one person over another in hiring/promoting, for example) based on irrelevant external characteristics. The idea is that you should not measure people by their flashy (for example) appearance or by how neat they dress. But, measure people by their character. You could say this is the Biblical passage Martin Luther King was alluding to in his famous "I have a dream" speech. For example, if you are responsible for selecting leadership for your company, you should read the verse several times for what you should be looking for (or should NOT be looking for) in leaders. Look at the Gospels and the type of people Jesus chose to build His Church, just fishermen (Matthew 4:18), regular people.[16] In CSR, companies should take into consideration all people impacted by the business, even the "lowly."

Exodus 23:1-9 emphasizes another aspect of fairness (the notion that we don't take advantage of people or take shortcuts to profit that take advantage of people[17]) towards all who are impacted by our

---

[15] "Freedom of conscience" has historically been an important quality supported by the western church, which focuses on the fact that people are constrained only by God in what they believe, not other people.

[16] But, certainly Paul became, we could say, the 13th disciple or 12th disciple (replacing Judas) who was "high speed" so to speak, the equivalent of an ivy league graduate, etc. (see Philippians 3:4-6). But Paul fully understood that his "credentials" were not the basis for his position: "But whatever gain I had, I counted as loss for the sake of Christ." (Philippians 3:7, ESV) The point is that God can and will use ALL types of people.

[17] Respect also means giving customers freedom to purchase what they want. For example, sales people have a responsibility to sell products or services. If, for

organization. The passage starts out, "You shall not spread a false report. You shall not join hands with a wicked man to be a malicious witness." (Exodus 23:1, ESV) This is how bad people survive. They accuse people in the way ("spread a false report") or pay people off (see Exodus 23:8) or they promise influence or position (see Proverbs 1:10 ff.). So, this makes people shift the truth and can result in others being treated unfairly. The Scripture really says "don't do that; it's a bad idea." Verse 2 continues, "You shall not fall in with many to do evil ..." (Exodus, 23:2, ESV). Notice that's the way that most people ("with many") go.[18] If we aren't alert to the negative people/community around us, we are just going to fall in step with everyone else in ignoring or mistreating others and the Scripture says again here in Exodus "don't do that" because it "perverts justice." (Exodus 23:2, ESV) God is a just God and we need to be meticulous about carrying out justice in business. Justice is important not only because it is the right thing to do, but it supports the entire economic system and brings honor to God. Great inefficiencies are introduced into markets through deceit and, we could argue (based on Exodus 23:2), spurious lawsuits.

Fairness also applies to how we handle people. Verse 3 says "nor shall you be partial to a poor man in his lawsuit ..." (Exodus 23:3, ESV), highlighting that justice works both ways.[19] Exodus 23:6 points out: "You shall not pervert the justice due to your poor in his lawsuit." (ESV) "The wicked" are not necessarily those with the most money,

---

example, a user only really needs a low-end computer, the sales person should make this recommendation, but if the customer insists on a higher-end version, the sales person should respect the customer's choice and sell them the high-end computer.

[18] As the New Testament tells us, "For the gate is narrow and the way is hard that leads to life, and those who find it are few" (Matthew 7:14, ESV) when it comes to genuine Biblical Christianity. So, the idea is that as a Christian, unless we have our minds in the game as the Scripture tells us (see Romans 12:2, Ephesians 4:17-18, Colossians 2:8), we can side with injustice.

[19] See also Leviticus 19:15, "You shall do no injustice in court. You shall not be partial to the poor or defer to the great, but in righteousness shall you judge your neighbor." (ESV)

but those who take advantage of other people (rich or poor).[20] "Keep far from a false charge ... And you shall take no bribe, for a bribe blinds the clear-sighted and subverts the cause of those who are in the right." (Exodus 23:8, ESV)

Deuteronomy highlights the need to work hard on fairness and respect, especially towards those who are most vulnerable. Deuteronomy 24:10 says "When you make your neighbor a loan of any sort, you shall not go into his house to collect his pledge." (ESV) Now "his pledge" is collateral and "You shall stand outside, and the man to whom you make the loan shall bring the pledge out to you." (Deuteronomy 24:11, ESV) Respect is the focus here. We expect the other person to do the right thing, even the poor, and hold them accountable, but without demeaning the person. Verse 14 continues, "You shall not oppress a hired worker who is poor and needy, whether he is one of your brothers or one of the sojourners who are in your land within your towns." (Deuteronomy 24:14, ESV) The passage never insinuates that hard work is the "oppression" but withholding of timely payment; "You shall give him his wages on the same day, before the sun sets (for he is poor and counts on it) ..." (Deuteronomy 24:15, ESV).

Continuing on with Deuteronomy 24:10-27, the principle of "gleaning" is perhaps the most important principle to consider for showing justice, at least as a starting point, when it comes to CSR programs. Look at Deuteronomy 24:19;

> When you reap your harvest in your field and forget a sheaf
> in the field, you shall not go back to get it. It shall be for the
> sojourner, the fatherless, and the widow, that the LORD
> your God may bless you in all the work of your hands. (ESV)

Deuteronomy 24:20 says the same thing about "olive trees" and "grapes of your vineyard." The idea is that in business, we don't have to squeeze

---

[20] See Nehemiah 5:4-5 where the government (at least in this case) is the primary agent of oppression.

every single bit of profit out of everything that we are doing, which is the realm of the finance function. Somehow we must leave some so that people can work to obtain the excess or the material you may not use. Now, the challenge is that in business, we talk about efficiency and this doesn't sound very efficient. But, the point is it blesses those who are in need. Also, there is nothing here that says that the company, or the farmer in this case, is putting all those stacks of excess grain, for example, or olives and hauling them to the village where the sojourners are just lying around in the shade; nothing like that. In fact, if you read the book of Ruth, which gives more insight maybe into this whole process, those who wanted the grain had to actually get out there and work hard to gather this excess.[21] So, for businesses, again avoiding this notion of paternalism, the focus is to allow people the opportunity to come secure what they need, not just providing things without any encouragement to work.[22] Because, if you recall from Genesis 1:26, work is fundamental to human dignity. And so, people are robbed of that dignity when we don't allow them the opportunity to work. But, it's done with respect.

Principle #3: Make Sure You Really Help

When we think of CSR, and the notion that somehow businesses need to "help" the community or "help" others, then the question becomes, "what does it really mean to help somebody"? As Christians, we need

---

[21] See Ruth 2:17-18a, "So she gleaned in the field until evening. Then she beat out what she had gleaned, and it was about an ephah of barley. And she took it up and went into the city." (ESV) Ruth started early in the morning and worked until evening gathering sheaves of barley. Then after working all day long, she removed the edible part from the sheaves and then carried the grain (about 22 liters worth) to her mother in law.

[22] Note Olasky's (1992) reference to earlier American attempts to help the poor (through providing workhouses for the indigent); "But enforcing work among the able-bodied was not seen as oppressive. The objective was to treat all as human beings, as members of the community with responsibilities, rather than as animals." (p. 11)

to understand what this means and what it doesn't mean or we're going to have problems, not only as the Church but as businesses as well. As Corbett and Fikkert (2012) point out:

> ... when North American Christians do attempt to alleviate poverty, the methods used often do considerable harm to both the materially poor and the materially non-poor. Our concern is not just that these methods are wasting ... resources but that these methods are actually exacerbating the very problems they are trying to solve. (p. 27)

Genesis 26:4 declares (written to Abraham) "I will multiply your offspring as the stars of heaven and will give to your offspring all these lands. And in your offspring *all the nations of the earth shall be blessed* ..." (ESV) (emphasis added). The principle for business is that God's people ought to bless everyone they do business with, both locally and globally.[23] But what does that mean and, specifically, how do you do it? We will answer with a specific list of items, but first let's look at some other Scriptures that give insights as to what it means (and doesn't mean) to "help."

Romans 1:16 reads; "For I am not ashamed of the gospel, for it is the power of God for salvation to everyone who believes, to the Jew first and also to the Greek." (ESV) Helping the poor involves reconciliation (and moving people in the right direction ethically), so God's Good News certainly can help.[24] Often times we simply look to material gifts

---

[23] See Jeremiah 29 where God's people in exile have found success and peace but God reminds them, "But seek the welfare of the city where I have sent you into exile, and pray to the LORD on its behalf, for in its welfare you will find your welfare." (Jeremiah 29:7, ESV)

[24] This means that we should do more than just giving immediate assistance. We need to "teach someone to fish" vs. just providing enough food for today. This is Jesus' point when He fed the 5,000 ... having a character (built through a relationship with the "Bread of Life") that can face and overcome difficulty is key to sustainable development. See 2 Timothy 2:2 which highlights the need to mentor individuals so they can then help others.

or education ("if they know more, they won't be poor") as "solutions" but (though helpful at points,[25]) they don't deal with the character and relationship restoration needed for long-term success.

As we look at Romans 15:1-3, "... weak" is not a vote for paternalism. We need to note the context gained from Romans 14, which is talking about a situation where a less mature believer thinks that what we eat impacts our spiritual status. More mature believers should know better (that what we eat does not impact our standing with God) and that these others are young in the faith; they're not as informed. So, we need to be considerate of this and maybe not eat the meat if they're concerned about it. So, when we talk about "infirmities," we don't mean that these people are helpless physically. It's actually referring to their beliefs and the fact that their beliefs are superficial (or we could say "uninformed" or "immature"). That's what "infirmities" means. It doesn't mean that we need to "bear up" with whatever people have going on in their lives. It means that we are to put up (in love) with people's misconceptions, which is again, not a blank check for paternalism. So to "help" someone does not mean that we do anything and everything for them because they are "weak."

Galatians 6:1-10 gives positive direction: "Bear one another's burdens, and so fulfill the law of Christ." (Galatians 6:2, ESV) So, the Biblical notion is that we are supposed to "bear one another's burdens." Now this focuses on the Church specifically. And the New Testament does emphasize that our first priority is to believers (Galatians 6:10) and then, also, as we read earlier in the Old Testament, as we have opportunity or as a situation presents itself (or faces us), we should help others as well. The whole point of bearing someone's burden is to help them get through a difficult situation so that they can go on and bear

---

[25] But, again, "education" (for example) is based on a worldview, so we need to ask "educating for what"? Depending on the purpose, "education" (as, for example, indoctrination) can also actually hurt.

their own burden[26] sooner than later.[27] It is never meant to say that we are to carry their load for ever and ever, unless of course in certain small cases; widows, orphans, the infirmed. But, for the vast majority of us, we should bear our own load. Because, "God is not mocked, for whatever one sows, that will he also reap ..." (Galatians 6:7, ESV). God has put us here to be productive[28] and to take care of the world that He gave us. So we do help when we come alongside someone to help them bear a difficult burden for a period of time (in most cases), so that they can continue on as a productive individual.

A primary principle in CSR programs is "don't contribute to the problem." If you are doing global business, for example, and there are unethical activities going on, don't participate in them. That's not being "the light of the world" (Matthew 5:14-15) and not helping anybody.

So what do we do? How do we help? Let's start by remembering Fikkert's (n.d.) definition of poverty which is "... broken relationships with God, self, others, and the rest of creation." As we seek reconciliation by helping, it is also important to clarify different types of helping

---

[26] The notion of personal responsibility has, historically, been an important part of western culture, but it is tempting to sacrifice personal freedom (which is precipitated on the notion of personal responsibility for choices) for short-term "peace" and "security." We could argue that Freud introduced this notion into culture with his application of the medical model to personal problems. If you have or "catch" a psychological "malady," how can you be responsible for it? Obviously, personal problems are often complex, but taking personal responsibility can be an important first step to solving the problem (i.e. see Alcoholic Anonymous' 12 steps).

See also Genesis 1:26-27, "And God said, 'Let us make man in our image, after our likeness: and let them have dominion over the fish of the sea, and over the fowl of the air, and over the cattle, and over all the earth, and over every creeping thing that creepeth upon the earth.'" (ESV)

[27] Note that Ephesians 4:16 suggests that we want others to "bear their own load" because everyone grows (including us) only when each individual part "is working properly" (ESV) or "as each part does its work" (NIV).

[28] Here "productive" is not simply an economic term (as the secularistic worldview might imply, see chapter 4 of this book) but a stewardship term. See, 1 Peter 4:10, "As each has received a gift, use it to serve one another, as good stewards of God's varied grace." (ESV) See also Matthew 25:14-30 where the focus is on using the talents God gave us.

based on the situation; relief, rehabilitation, or development (Corbett & Fikkert, 2012).

Leviticus gives one specific way to help and that is to pay poorer workers promptly and do not ridicule the handicapped, "The wages of a hired worker shall not remain with you all night until the morning. You shall not curse the deaf or put a stumbling block before the blind, but you shall fear your God: I am the Lord." (ESV) As we mentioned above, this shows consideration of the immediate financial obligations and possible physical limitations of a vulnerable citizen.

Another part of helping is making sure you focus on the right people to help. The Scripture highlights several groups of people who are the most vulnerable in society: widows, orphans and "sojourners"[29] and others who are poor "through no fault of their own."[30] See Deuteronomy 24:17 that reads, "'You shall not pervert the justice due to the sojourner or to the fatherless, or take a widow's garment in pledge ...'" (ESV).

When it comes to social responsibility and business, the company should scan and see if there is anything that they can do to address an obvious problem in the community and just do it. Now, again, this looks like (according to Exodus 23:4-5) one-time help, not on-going help; which we'll come back to.

Olasky (1992) presents "the seven marks of compassion" as a way to really help in communities. But he prefaces his comments by highlighting what compassion is NOT, as he describes the community efforts to help the poor in the mid to late 1800s in the United States.

> [The secret of their success] ... was not neglect, either benign
> or malign; ... Nor was the secret of their success a century
> ago the showering of money on the poor, nor the triumph

---

[29] A "sojourner" was a gentile convert, someone who was not a normal part of the predominate group. Immigrants or those who are "new in town" might qualify as well in modern terms.

[30] So, there seems to be little precedent in Scripture for organizations that focus on "raising awareness" as their mission versus actually doing something for someone; but a complex issue.

of an antistatist spirit; they knew that private agencies could be just as bad as government ones. (p. 101) (brackets added)

The seven principles that seemed to help show real help to those in need are: Affiliation, Bonding, Categorization, Discernment, Employment and Freedom (Olasky, 1992). Let's take a closer look at each one.

Affiliation means that you have to put people in contact with those they are naturally connected to; their families, churches, fraternal/ ethnic groups, communities. In order to figure out how to help people, we need to figure out who (including which institution) is best suited to do what. An historical example sheds light.

> In practice, when individuals or families with real needs applied for material assistance, charity workers began by interviewing applicants and checking backgrounds in order to answer one question: "Who is bound to help in this case"? Charity workers then tried to call in relatives, neighbors, or former coworkers or coworshippers. (Olasky, 1992, p. 102)

As Corbett and Fikkert (2012) point out,

> Finally, no single sector can alleviate poverty on its own. Like all human beings, poor people have a range of physical, emotional, social, and spiritual needs. Hence, appropriate interventions for poor people include such diverse sectors as economic development, health, education, agriculture, spiritual formation, etc. (p. 14)

And affinity groups have the best chance of providing the needed help. Since this is the case, let's explore in more detail the proper role of institutions in helping.

> Furthermore, the institutional context greatly influences both the type and scale of various poverty-alleviation

efforts. Some Christians [or businesses] are called to work at a government level, seeking to promote justice for the poor through public policy. Others are called to work in the business world where they can provide job opportunities for the unemployed. (Corbett & Fikkert, 2012, p. 14) (brackets added)

Christians can work through church or parachurch ministries and also as individuals (helping a neighbor in need). Since families are the primary institution for affiliation,[31] if you're trying to help someone, first find out about their family and how their family can help them. Church and community and family are primary institutions and businesses should try to partner with these groups if they really want to help. That's why, I think, organizations need to be concerned about families as their primary CSR responsibility; to be encouraging families, building families as God intended. Government plays an important role by setting up just laws and then enforcing them fairly (Romans 13:1-7). We also help as individuals. "Each Christian has a unique set of gifts, callings, and responsibilities that influence the scope and manner in which to fulfill the Biblical mandate to help the poor." (Corbett & Fikkert, 2012, p. 13)

Bonding highlights that changing people is a relational effort, not just a financial one. "The key [to helping the poor] was personal willingness to become deeply involved." (Olasky, 1992, p. 104) (brackets added) So volunteers (i.e. from companies) can do more than push paper or help with landscaping but can have "... a narrow but deep responsibility ..." (Olasky, 1992, p. 103) to build relationships with those who are truly alone. As Olasky notes (1992), "The key [to successful help] was a

---

[31] See Genesis 2:18, 24; "Then the LORD God said, 'It is not good that man should be along; I will make him a helper fit for him.' ... Therefore a man shall leave his father and his mother and hold fast to his wife, and the two shall become one flesh." (ESV) The primary purpose of marriage/family is companionship for the man and woman. Thus family is designed by God from Creation to be the primary means for meeting our desire for companionship.

personal willingness to become deeply involved ... good charity could not be based on the 'overworked and somewhat mechanical offices of a relieving society.'" (p. 104) (brackets added)

The next recommendation of what it means to really help cuts against the grain of modern culture, but nevertheless needs to be understood for what it means, and that is *Categorization*.[32] Categorization of individuals can help charity organizations match the right people and solutions with the right person in need. For example, historically;

> ... charity organization societies considered "worthy of relief" only those who were poor through no fault of their own and unable to change their situation quickly. In this category were orphans, the aged, the incurably ill, children with "one parent unable to support them," and adults suffering from "temporary illness or accident." Volunteers who were tender-hearted but not particularly forceful served as helpers to the helpless. (Olasky, 1992, p. 104)

Other individuals who were able to work were sent to employment bureaus and classified as "Needing Work Rather Than Relief." (Olasky, 1992) But the "shiftless and deceitful" who were able but unwilling to work were classified as "Unworthy, Not Entitled to Relief." However, this group was not necessarily refused consideration but volunteers who worked with this group "... had to be of hardy stock and often of rough experience; the best were often [former] alcoholics or ex-convicts."

---

[32] However, historically this had not been the case. As Aristotle (circa. 340 B.C.) pointed out, "And not only are mental diseases voluntary, but the bodily are so in some men, whom we accordingly blame: for such as are naturally deformed no one blames, only such as are so by reason of want of exercise, and neglect: and so too of weakness and maiming: no one would think of upbraiding, but would rather compassionate, a man who is blind by nature, or from disease, or from an accident; but every one would blame him who was so from excess of wine, or any other kind of intemperance." See examples that follow and discriminating between someone who has issues through "no fault of their own" vs. someone who has a "disability" through neglect.

(Olasky, 1992, p. 105) (brackets added) A "work test" was often the best way to determine how to classify individuals and might be something to consider today.[33]

In the discussion of this principle, it is helpful to clarify what is meant by *relief* and its reciprocal – *development*. Let's start with relief. "Relief can be defined as the urgent and temporary provision of emergency aid to reduce immediate suffering from a natural or man-made crisis." (Corbett & Fikkert, 2012, p. 99) So, relief is short-term and, we could argue, focused on basic, immediate material needs; food, clothing (and shelter) and possibly safety. The key issue here is that the recipient must truly have no ability to help themselves. It is like the Good Samaritan "bandaging ... the helpless man who lay bleeding along the roadside." (Corbett & Fikkert, 2012, p. 100) Rehabilitation (an intermediary step from relief to development), "... begins as soon as the bleeding stops; it seeks to restore people and their communities to the positive elements of their pre-crisis conditions." (Corbett & Fikkert, 2012, p. 100) In this step, the helper works with those in need to move them and their community forward to restoration (Corbett & Fikkert, 2012). Finally,

> *Development* is a process of ongoing change that moves all the people involved – both the *helpers* and the *helped* – closer to being in right relationship with God, self, others, and the rest of creation. In particular, as the materially poor develop, they are better able to fulfill their calling of glorifying God by working and supporting themselves and their families with the fruits of their work. Development is not done to or *for* people but *with* people. (Corbett & Fikkert, 2012, p. 100)

It is helpful to keep these three categories in mind when analyzing different helping opportunities and how best to deliver that help. Corbett & Fikkert (2012) remind us of the seriousness of this step:

---

[33] A point we have made in the book is that work is not demeaning but actually an important part of who we are as human beings.

It is absolutely crucial that we determine whether relief, rehabilitation, or development is the appropriate intervention:

> **One of the biggest mistakes that North American churches [and we could add business CSR programs] make – by far – is in applying relief in situations in which rehabilitation or development is the appropriate intervention.** (p. 101) (brackets added)

Discernment (or "benign suspicion") follows naturally here, which means knowing people and knowing the Scriptural point of view about them. Charity workers historically noted that some "'preferred their condition and even tried to take advantage of it' ... [and] that [the] ... 'duplication of alms [was] pursued with cunning and attended most invariably with deceit and falsehood.'" (Olasky, 1992, p. 107) (brackets added) This is why, for example, affinity is important so that information can be confirmed or exposed, and bonding provides the relationship needed to hold someone accountable in love.[34] "Discernment by volunteers, and organizational barriers against fraud, were important not only to prevent waste but to preserve morale among those who were working hard to remain independent." (Olasky, 1992, p. 107) Discernment also excludes "indiscriminate giving" which was described as "not mercy" and "positively immoral." (Olasky, 1992)

Long term *Employment* is also a critical long-term way to help which (as we discuss in chapter 7) businesses do inherently. Wood yards and sewing rooms usually accompanied earlier (1800s) charity centers so that those receiving assistance paid their way. As was said, "New York charity leader Josephine Lowell wrote, 'the problem before those who

---

[34] See Romans 15:14, "I myself am satisfied about you, my brothers, that you yourselves are full of goodness, filled with all knowledge and able to instruct one another." (ESV) This verse (based on Greek word for "instruct" which is *noutheo*) gives a framework for the accountability needed; which involves confrontation with humility, real loving concern, and specific pointers for change. For more, see "What is 'Nouthetic' Counseling?" from: www.nouthetic.com (see *About INS*).

would be charitable, is not how to deal with a given number of poor; it is how to help those who are poor, without adding to their numbers and constantly increasing the evils they seek to cure.'" (Olasky, 1992, p. 110) So, work was seen as a pathway out of poverty.

Finally, *Freedom* should be the long-term goal as employment is achieved. Freedom was understood by immigrants, historically, "... not as the opportunity to do anything with anyone at any time, but as the opportunity to work and worship without governmental restriction." (Olasky, 1992, p. 111) However, freedom does not necessarily happen immediately but comes from hard work and sacrifice. As was said, "Charity leaders and preachers frequently spoke of freedom and showed how dependency [especially to governmental welfare] was merely slavery with a smiling mask ... [and] Freedom could be grasped only when individuals took responsibility." (Olasky, 1992, p. 112) (brackets added)

Principle #4: Beware of Corrupt People and Organizations

1 Timothy 6:8 reads; "But if we have food and clothing, with these we will be content. But those who desire to be rich fall into temptation." (ESV) This passage gives perspective on what we really need (food and clothing/shelter), but also insinuates that "helping the poor" and "seeking social justice" can provide a vehicle for greed and manipulation for the purpose of gaining personal and/or political power. So organizations must be alert![35]

1 Peter 5:2-3 intimates that money and power can be the driving motive for people being involved in "preaching" or "helping" by contrasting proper leadership (real helping) with what is phony, "...

---

[35] See Ephesian 6:10-11 where God tells us to "... be strong in the Lord and in the strength of his might. Put on the whole armor of God that you may be able to stand against the schemes of the devil." (ESV) It should not be surprising the individuals and groups who present themselves as wanting to "help" can hold nefarious motives. See 2 Corinthians 11:12-15, "... For such men are false apostles, deceitful workmen, disguising themselves as apostles of Christ. And no wonder for even Satan disguises himself as an angel of light." (ESV)

shepherd the flock of God that is among you, ... not for shameful gain ... not domineering over those in your charge ...” (ESV).[36] So, this passage assumes that in some cases people secure leadership positions or, in our case, non-profits (NGOs or not for profits) or governmental positions, primarily for personal financial gain and/or power. Philippians 1:15-17 confirms this potential problem, “Some indeed preach Christ from envy and rivalry ... The former proclaim Christ out of selfish ambition ...” (ESV). Envy involves anger at someone who is more talented than you and/or has a higher position and is doing well. In its fullest form, it can lead to more than anger, but an active desire to punish and “take down” the “offending party.”[37] For example, the Sanhedrin (religious governmental officials) and high priest wanted Jesus killed due to envy, “For he [Pilate] knew that it was out of envy that they had delivered him up [to be killed].” (Matthew 27:18, ESV) (brackets added)

This love of money through dishonest (often through manipulation by appearing to be wanting to “help” others) gain is equated with the “sin of Balaam” who committed a particularly heinous offense in the Old Testament. He was a prophet who was positioned to help people, but merely used his position for his own selfish gain, “Forsaking the right way, they have gone astray. They have followed the way of Balaam, the son of Peor, who loved gain from wrongdoing ...” (2 Peter 2:15, ESV). People have mixed motives for wanting your money and or

---

[36] See also 1 Timothy 3:8 where candidates for the office of Deacon must “... not [be] greedy for dishonest gain.” (ESV) (brackets added); thus indicating that being greedy for dishonest gain can be a tendency, even in the church. Titus 1:7 reminds that a potential Elder must not be “greedy for gain.” (ESV)

[37] “*Resentiment* is a larger form of envy or jealousy ... in making comparisons, with others, it is not enough to resent another’s status or accomplishments but leads to determined effort to destroy that individual.” (Schlossberg, 1993, p. 52) See an example in the book of Esther where the goal is not only to punish a successful individual but all his people, “And when Haman saw that Mordecai did not bow down or pay homage to him, Haman was filled with fury. But he disdained to lay hands on Mordecai alone. So, as they had made known to him the people of Mordecai, Haman sought to destroy all the Jews, the people of Mordecai, throughout the whole kingdom of Ahasuerus.” (Esther 3:5-6, ESV)

showing "concern" for the poor. So we need to be alert to this when determining who to invest in.[38]

Principle #5: Take Care of the Environment

Now, what about the environment? We cannot cover the topic in detail, but can at least suggest a few important basic principles. Genesis 3:17-19 reminds us that nature is cursed because of the sin of Adam and Eve; "... cursed is the ground because of you ..." (Genesis 3:17, ESV). But, God's Creation is good. Romans 8:18-27 gives much more detail on exactly what happened to the environment and ramifications for now and the future. First of all, nature is "looking" for redemption that can only come ultimately from God because it is God's creation, "For the creation waits with eager longing for the revealing of the sons of God ... that the creation itself will be set free from the bondage to corruption and obtain the freedom of the glory of the children of God." (Romans 8:20-21, ESV) So, environmentalism is not an end, but a result of God's work and God eventually establishing "... a new heaven and a new earth ..." (Revelations 21:1, ESV).

As God's people, we need to be redeeming nature as well; which means taking care of it, using it well and enjoying its beauty, and certainly not polluting or trashing nature or misusing God's resources. Christians should excel in this area because it reflects our respect for God. But, 1 Corinthians 15:39 reminds us that we are not the same as the rest of nature, "For not all flesh is the same, but there is one kind for humans, another for animals, another for birds, and another for fish." (ESV) It basically says that there are different kinds of flesh; there is a flesh of animals, there is a flesh of people.[39] In summary,

---

[38] "Altruism is thus best interpreted as a counterfeit of Christian love, informed by the ideology of humanism and powered by resentment. It permits demeaning the successful, or those who display any form of superiority, by pulling over that act the mask of concern for the poor and weak." (Schlossberg, 1993, p. 53)

[39] So, it dispels the Naturalistic notion that people are just evolved from animals. And it dispels the Eastern monistic notion that nature is "one" with God.

Genesis 1:26 reminds us that God wants us to take care of the world that we live in.

When it comes to organizations and the environment, accountability and frugality are important. In other words, we want to be *accountable* to others which makes us think about the waste that we are putting into the environment because it impacts others and also, mainly because we are not taking care of the world that God called us to take care of, which is the bigger problem. *Frugality* involves using God's resources in nature as efficiently as possible. This quality respects God's creation but also allows companies to make more money. If you think about it, waste is a cost. If you can use that waste (or eliminate it) for some kind of product that you can sell and gain some kind of financial return for it (or at least forego the cost of it), then the company and the environment are much better off. This requires businesses to adopt in-house procedures and purchasing practices that make effective use of God's resources with the goal being zero waste.

The world belongs to God, so we should enjoy it but also take care of it and the people in it. As Psalm 24:1 says; "The earth is the LORD's and the fullness thereof, the world and those who dwell therein, ..." (Psalm 24:1, ESV). We are responsible for taking care of nature and need to work hard to do so (Genesis 2:15), using our unique gifts (1 Peter 4:10).

PROGRAM POINTS

We have discussed basic CSR guiding principles (including warnings). Now, let's get specific. Exactly what should go into a helpful CSR program for organizations?

Matthew 25:35 ff. describes the actions of those who reflect God's compassion and in the process, give specific areas of focus that should be included in a CSR program; "... 'For I was hungry and you gave me food, I was thirsty and you gave me drink, I was a stranger and you welcomed me, I was naked and you clothed me, I was in prison and you came to me.'" (Matthew 25:35-37, ESV) So CSR programs that make a difference include meeting basic needs; food (and drink) and shelter (clothing) as well as relationship and justice to those who are defenseless (the "stranger") or in prison (but with discernment). You can see that these categories seem to reflect needed relief[40] and possible rehabilitation (see Principle #3 above), but not necessarily development.[41] So, one aspect of a helpful CSR program includes having a disaster plan that not only includes its employees but also people in the community, as appropriate. Here is a list of other, specific program points for companies:

- Work through partnerships, but;
  - Make sure what they mean by "helping" is what you intend
  - Make sure the potential partner supports the same values as you
  - Check financials. A rule of thumb is that a good non-profit only uses a maximum of 20% or less of donations towards administration and the rest goes directly to helping people. Also a rule of thumb is that the salary of a CEO of a non-profit should be around (more or less) $75,000 [based on interview with a non-profit CEO].
- Be strategic, not nepotistic
- Connect people you are trying to help to institutions that are closest to them.

---

[40] See Genesis 45:4-8 which summarizes how Joseph took action to provide relief not only for the people of Egypt for that part of the world. It also encourages individuals, companies and governments to hold surpluses for potential difficult situations.

[41] That is why we could argue that organizations that boast about how much, for example, food they deliver is really meaningless information. It is more helpful to know about the specific people who receive the food and whether or not they have a genuine need for relief or if they be working to secure the food. This is an important point because organizations (particularly large companies) are meant to feel guilty because they "have so much" so may be pressured to simply give out of false guilt rather than having the courage to understand and execute a CSR program that really helps.

- Pursue justice for those who are exploited through your own business practices and, if possible, through legal means (formal or informal)
- If clearly stated in corporate documents, it is OK to give (as charity) corporate funds to specific groups, but it should be fully disclosed to investors. A potentially better approach for charity is a matching program where the donations of individuals in the company are matched by the company, which allows for maximum freedom.
- Consider giving employees five hours a month to become involved in community service with an organization of their choice (within parameters).

Let's examine these program points and other aspects of setting up and running an effective CSR program in more detail. First of all, businesses do more good than most acknowledge by providing jobs.[42] But companies still need to "do good" by everyone they do business with.

Companies need to have a long-term perspective. Companies highlighted by "get-rich-quick," as we've seen from our earlier readings from Ecclesiastes and Proverbs, many not last. As the Scripture says "For what does it profit a man if he gains the whole world and loses or forfeits himself?" (Luke 9:25, ESV) So we want to take those organizational values, like integrity, and use in the community. You also need to be concerned about your suppliers and contractors (at home and abroad) as well as others you do business with.

Regarding "Be strategic, not nepotistic;" *nepotism* means that you get involved with a certain organization and/or project just because someone in your organization knows somebody. So, you may not think strategically about what is the right thing to do based on your community and your situation (what you can best offer) and your values.

Be wise in partnering with non-profits. We learn from Scripture (see previous section) that people can use "good" causes for personal

---

[42] We could argue that the best way to help the poor is to start a business.

gain; whether personal wealth, prestige and/or power for themselves or their cause. As you approach a non-profit or NGO (non governmental organization),[43] you shouldn't have to give up your organizational standards to work with them. There doesn't have to be a conflict between concern for the community and the environment and making money. Provide relief in crises, but the goal is that people can be self-sustaining. The best we can do for CSR is to identify secondary stakeholders and examine the company's responsibility to each one while fulfilling fiduciary obligations ethically to primary stakeholders.[44]

Work through partnerships. Use organizations and people who are capable and are better equipped to help. Here is where you have to do your homework and here is where companies break down and why Christians should really be front and center in helping companies discover partners that really help people. Make sure your partner supports the same values as you.[45] Also, check the financials of the organization you want to partner with (as noted above). Seek out smaller non-profits who may be more effective in helping. Stand strong against coercion.[46] Know the difference between *Relief* and *Development* (see above) and be prepared for both for your own people and the community. Encourage institutions that do help. Cooperate with government, but be very aware of conflicts of interest. Work with government based on their role in keeping the law (i.e. helping provide safety in an impoverished neighborhood and making sure the legal system upholds justice). The main thing is to give thought to the program! "It would indeed be tragic if companies valiantly responded to the call by many to imbed CSR in their corporate approach only to find out that they are not really helping

---

[43] It is better if companies are proactive in approaching groups to partner with that match their purposes versus simply just reacting to whatever group approaches them.

[44] See Ruddell's et al. (2012) article on ethics and illegal aliens.

[45] For example companies should not feel obligated (out of "guilt" or pressure) to support organizations that are anti-business.

[46] This includes non-profit or governmental entities who might pressure you to support them through threat of activism against you, so becomes a *de facto* bribe.

those whom they purport to help but in some cases may actually be causing harm." (Olasky, Oliver, & Pambianco, 1991)

Donohue (2011) reflects our earlier material when it comes to assessing whether an initiative helps or not but takes it from the perspective of the organization. In this context, she coaches organizations to focus on *input* versus *output*.

> What's an output conversation? It is when you talk about your Good Work Output For example:

> - We have invested $20,000 dollars in X
> - We have 50 employees who donated X amount of Hours volunteering
> - We have helped 37 charities this year

> All of these our output numbers – and the problem with them is that they don't build trust. My research indicates that in fact these numbers can hurt your business and weaken consumer trust. (Donohue, 2011)

Donohue does a good job of questioning what it means to actually "do good" from an organizational assessment side. She goes on to point out a better way to assess whether or not CSR initiatives help the company.

> Input numbers are numbers that can measure the value of the good the company is doing. In my first study the input numbers we used were staff satisfaction, media counts and consumer trust in the brand. Inputs are the outcomes you want your giving to affect. Yes – your giving should have an effect on your business – because if it does not – it [your business but also the CSR program itself] will not be sustainable and as we have seen over the last three years when corporate giving isn't sustained communities suffer. When

communities suffer brands suffer and when brands suffer profits suffer. (Donohue, 2011) (brackets added)

Donohue focuses on the business model for CSR (it is "good for business"), so it makes sense to do it right. I would not disagree and venture that the other part of the equation holds true, that when people are really helped (as we discussed in earlier section) it reflects well on the business in the long run.

In summary, God made His Covenant with Abraham "and His offspring." God said He would bless Abraham and His seed so that he (we) could be "a blessing [to the nations]" (Genesis 12:2, ESV) (brackets added). As we are blessed materially or otherwise, we have an obligation to seek ways to bless others!

CHAPTER 7 QUESTIONS FOR REVIEW

1. How would you analyze the term *corporate social responsibility*? What questions do you have about the meaning of the words? What might be an alternative term?

2. What is a way to define "poverty" from a Christian worldview? What ramifications does this understanding have for how we approach CSR?

3. Give one or two verses that encourage us to help the poor.

4. What does 2 Corinthians 9:6-7 have to say about CSR?

5. Explain James 2:1-17 and what it says about fairness.

6. Describe the Old Testament concept of "gleaning." Give a reference. How might this principle guide company CSR efforts?

7. Describe Galatians 6:1-10 and what it has to say about helping others.

8. Describe two or three negative qualities to be aware of when you seek to partner with other non-profit or governmental entities.

9. List and describe the stakeholders in your own workplace (or a future one). How does your organization address the importance of each stakeholder group?

10. Discuss the practice of corporate philanthropy (giving) in your organization or what you would like to see in an organization.

FINAL THOUGHT

My brother Jim has worked with several different engineering firms during the course of his career. He has done very well and his company on a number of occasions has entrusted him with the responsibility of serving on the bid team for obtaining new work (with millions of dollars at stake) for his company. During one of these bid meetings, he had an interesting experience.[47] It was the last meeting before the final presentation to the customer as to why his company could do the best job of performing the project. They were competing with one other firm for the contract. Toward the end of the discussion, one of the members of the bid team threw out a statement: "I wonder what the other company will present tomorrow." Slowly the idea caught on and gained momentum. Another volunteered, "Yes I know someone who can give us information from the other company." Others chimed in, "yeah, let's find out exactly what the other guys will bid, so that we can make sure our bid will win." Finally, the parallel flashed through my brother's brain. He spoke, "What you are saying is interesting. It is kind of like what they did at Watergate. You know we are going to win this bid. We don't need to stoop to this level and jeopardize our efforts." Slowly but surely the rest of the committee sheepishly nodded and the potential unethical deed was laid to rest. Sure enough, they did win the bid, fair and square.

---

[47] This depiction is not exact. It has been generalized and changed but carries the original significance.

This is what this book is all about; knowing your ethics so well that you naturally act on them in real situations, no matter what your position in the organization. In doing so, you **are** a leader. The result is that you **will** make a profit in the long run by carrying out business in the ethical way. What are you going to do? It gets down to real people like you taking real action in real situations. I hope that you soar as one who influences individuals and business institutions for good. This is **real** leadership. This is our calling. This is how business ethics works.

APPENDIX A

HERE IS A SAMPLE ORGANIZATIONAL ethics statement based on what we have covered in the book. Note, that this ethics statement answers the two questions; (1) "What are your standards"? (see the five ethical standards listed below for the answer to the first question) and (2) "Where did they come from"? (see the "We believe" statement which articulates the worldview for the standards)

You would then develop your "Code of Conduct" by addressing particular ethical issues that the people in your company face and then detailing what you want your people NOT to do and, more importantly, what you want them TO DO (based on standards laid out in your ethics statement) when faced with those situations.

SAMPLE ETHICS STATEMENT

We believe,

- that ethical standards do not change but the application of those standards does change. Therefore, we will hold firm to our standards, but constantly learn and grow in how to apply these standards at the organizational, process, and personal level. Because these standards do not change, no one in the organization (including the CEO and Board) can overturn these standards. The standards dictate behavior. Behavior or shifting beliefs do not dictate the standards.

- that to have a successful company for a long period of time, we must run it in an ethical manner. We realize that not everyone is ethical, so we will be wise in how we carry out business with all our constituents because we don't want good people affected in a negative way. We will take care to hire people who can accept our standards so they will be fulfilled while working with us instead of frustrated. We will be careful to treat everyone fairly (according to our adopted standards), but we will take corrective action against unethical behavior.
- that to have a highly ethical company does not mean that we will be legalistic. The bureaucracy does not uphold ethics, individuals do. So, we will be careful to set up structures that uphold our high standards without becoming legalistic and hindering creativity and individuality.

We hold these five ethical standards based on a committed relationship between the company leaders and employees and all parties affected by our business:

1. **Have a long term, big picture perspective**

   This is essential to business ethics. We don't want to sacrifice our long-term success for an unethical, immediate deal. What we fail to consider is that the unethical deal has ramifications for future business; it can harm business in the long run. We are confident that if we focus on carrying out business in an ethical way and doing good to our customers that we will be very successful financially in the long run.

2. **Be honest**

   We will communicate openly and honestly to those who need to hear.

3. **Be wise**

We will implement a system of checks and balances to hold people accountable, including upper level management and the Board of Directors, to the organizational standards detailed in this ethics statement. We will trust people but we will check everything.

4. **Be diligent**

All members of the organization will work hard with an understanding of the purpose of the work. As the company prospers from this hard work, then those who work hard will benefit. At times, members of our organization will face difficulty. We want to help each other through these difficulties so that all of us can continue with our hard work. In this way, the company will gain the most profit. Those who do not share the hard work will not share in the profits of the organization.

5. **Do good to people**

We want to intentionally do good to all of the people with whom we do business including employees, customers, vendors, stockholders, and the community around us. As our company does well, we want to wisely share our surplus with others.

REFERENCES

Adams, J. (1983). Preaching to the heart. Phillipsburg, NJ: Presbyterian and Reformed Publishing Company.

Alinsky, S. D. (1971). Rules for radicals. New York, NY: Vintage Books.

Amaeshiand, K. M., & Adi, B. (2007). Reconstructing the corporate social responsibility construct in Utlish. *Business Ethics: A European Review*, 16, 3-18.

Aristotle. (circa 340 BC). Ethics. Produced by Garvin, T., Widger, D, & the DP Team.

Barclay, W. (1959). The daily bible study series. the letters to the Philippians, Colossians, and Thessalonians. Philadelphia, PA: Westminster Press.

Barclay, W. (1975). The daily bible study series: the letters to Timothy, Titus, and Philemon. Philadelphia, PA: Westminster Press.

Belz, J. (2001, October 27). Tolerance vs. pluralism. *World Magazine*.

Blamires, H. (1963). The Christian mind. Ann Arbor, MI: Servant Books.

Blanchard, K., & Peale, N. V. (1988). The power of ethical management. New York, NY: William Morrow and Company, Inc.

Bowie, N. E. (1998, January). Companies are discovering the value of ethics. *USA Today (*Magazine*)*, 126(2632), Retrieved from www.findarticles.com.

Bradley, R. L. (2009). Capitalism at work: business, government and energy. Ontario: M & M Scrivener Press..

Burkett, L. (1990). Business by the book. Nashville, TN: Thomas Nelson Publishers.

Campbell, M. (n.d.). Clean up or pay up. Retrieved from www. ABCNEWS.com.

Caterpillar. (2010). Our values in action. Retrieved from http://www. caterpillar.com/en/company/code-of-conduct.html.

Cavanagh, G. F. (1998). American business values with international perspectives. Upper Saddle River, NJ: Prentice Hall.

Chappell, T. (1993). The soul of a business. New York, NY: Bantam Books.

Chappell, T. (1999). Managing upside down. New York, NY: William Morrow and Company, Inc.

Chewning, R. C., Eby, J. W., & Roels, S. J. (1990). Business through the eyes of faith. San Francisco, CA: Harper.

Collins, J. C., & Porras, J. I. (2002). Built to last. New York, NY: Harper Business Essentials.

Corbett, S., & Fikkert, B. (2012). When helping hurts. Chicago, IL: Moody Publishers.

De Pree, M. (1989). Leadership is an art. New York, NY: Doubleday.

Donohue, M. (2011). CSR assessment. Lecture conducted from Indianapolis, IN.

Douglass, E., & Rutten, T. (2002, January 30). Accounting worried global crossing exec. *Los Angeles Times*.

Driscoll, D., Hoffman, W. M., & Petry, E. S. (1995). The ethical edge. New York, NY: MasterMedia Limited.

Dylan, B. (2008). Gotta serve somebody. Retrieved from http://www. youtube.com/watch?v=icUVZHRi3ps.

Etzioni, A. (2002, August 4). When it comes to ethics, b-schools get an F. Retrieved from www.WashingtonPost.com.

Ford, D. J. (2003). In the name of God, amen: rediscovering Biblical and historical covenants. St. Louis, MI: Lex Rex Publishing.

Friedman, M. (1962). Capitalism and freedom. Chicago, IL: The University of Chicago Press.

Gehrman, D. H. (2003). View from the bridge: what's your number? Unpublished manuscript.

George, R. P. (2001). The clash of orthodoxies. Wilmington, DE: ISI Books.

Guy, M. E. (1990). Decision making in everyday work situations. New York, NY: Quorom Books.

Hendricksen, W. (1957). New testament commentary series: I-II Timothy and Titus. Grand Rapids, MI: Baker Book House.

Kidner, D. (1976). A time to mourn and a time to dance. Downers Grove, IL: InterVarsity Press.

Kaiser, Jr., W. C. (1978). Toward an Old Testament theology. Grand Rapids, MI: Zondervan Publishing House.

Kant, I. (1889). Fundamental principles of the metaphysics of morals. (T. K. Abbott, Trans). London: Longmans, Green, & Co. (Original work published 1785).

Kurtz, P. (Ed.). (1973). Humanist manifesto I and II. Buffalo, NY: Prometheus Books.

Lewis, C. S. (1952). Mere Christianity. San Francisco, CA: Harper.

Manz, C. C., Manz, K. P., Marx, R. D., & Neck, C. P. (2001). The wisdom of Solomon at work. San Francisco, CA: Berrett-Koehler Publishers, Inc.

McDonald, O. (1978). Christian ethics. In J. D. Douglas (Ed.), The new international dictionary of the Christian church, revised edition. Grand Rapids, MI: Zondervan.

McNamara, C. (2000). Complete guide to ethics management: an ethics toolkit for managers. Retrieved from www.mapnp.org/library/ethics/ethxgde.htm.

Mill, J. S. (1879). Utilitarianism. Reprinted from *Fraser's Magazine*, 7th edition. London: Longman, Green, and Co.

Murray, F. (2002, February 11). Shades of Enron at Global Crossing. *The Washington Times*.

Niebuhr, R. H. (1975). Christ and culture. New York, NY: Harper Colophon Books, Harper & Row Publishers.

Olasky, M., Oliver, D. T., & Pambianco, R. V. (1991). Patterns of corporate philanthropy: funding false compassion. In W. T. Poole (Ed.), Studies in philanthropy #9. Washington, D.C.: Capital Research Center.

Olasky, M. (1992). The tragedy of American compassion. Wheaton, IL: Crossway Books.

Pava, M. (2003). Leading with meaning. New York, NY: Palgrave Macmillan.

Rae, S. B., & Wong, K. L. (1996). Beyond integrity: a Judeo-Christian approach to business ethics. Grand Rapids, MI: Zondervan Publishing House.

Robertson, O. P. (1987). Covenants: God's way with his people. Philadelphia, PA: Great Commission Publications.

Ruddell, L. S. (1992). *Values of key leaders and how they relate to organizational culture.* (Unpublished doctoral dissertation). University of Houston, Houston, TX.

Ruddell, L. S., Champion, W., & Norris, D. (2012). The ethical dilemma of local ordinances that purport to deport illegal aliens. *University of Detroit – Mercy Law Review*, 89, 299-314.

Ruddell, L. S. (2014). Corporate social responsibility: helping students understand the historical and modern construct for future results. Proceedings from *MMA Fall Educators' Conference – 2014*. San Antonio, TX. Retrieved from http://www.mmaglobal. org/publications/proceedings-archive/.

Sainsbury, H. (1978). Moral theology. In J. D. Douglas (Ed.), The new international dictionary of the Christian church, Revised edition. Grand Rapids, MI: Zondervan.

Schaeffer, F. (1968). The God who is there. Chicago, IL: InterVarsity Press.

Schaeffer, F. (2006). Escape from reason. Chicago, IL: InterVarsity Press.

Schlossberg, H. (1993). Idols for destruction. Wheaton, IL: Crossway Books.

Schwartz, M., & Watkins, S. (2003). Power failure. New York, NY: Doubleday.

Sire, J. W. (1976). The universe next door. Downers Grove, IL: InterVarsity Press.

Sire, J. W. (1990). Discipleship of the mind. Downers Grove, IL: InterVarsity Press.

Smith, A. (1759). The theory of moral sentiments. Reprint. Indianapolis, IN: Liberty Press.

Sproul, R.C. (1986). Ethics and the Christian. Wheaton, IL: Tyndale House Publishers, Inc.

Sproul, R.C. (1993). Battle for our minds. Orlando, FL: Ligonier Ministries.

Stayton, W. (1983). Ethics and values. Unpublished manuscript.

Strauss, G. (1992). Christianity and culture: the case for reformational cultural activism. Retrieved from http://thebigpicture. homestead.com/files/CHRISTIANITYANDCULTURE.html

Thompson, J.A. (1974). Deuteronomy: an introduction and commentary. Downers Grove, IL: InterVarsity Press.

Tucker, R. C. (Ed.). (1978). The Marx-Engels reader, 2nd edition. New York, NY: W.W. Norton & Company.

Ward, R. A. (1974). Commentary on 1 and 2 Timothy and Titus. Waco, TX: Word Books.

Whitehead, J. (1982). The second great American revolution. Elgin, IL: David C. Cook.

Wood, P. (2003). Diversity: the invention of a concept. San Francisco, CA: Encounter Books.